THE ISLE OF SKYE
A Walker's Guide

Marsco from the summit of Bla Bheinn

THE ISLE OF SKYE
A Walker's Guide

Peace be to thee and thy children, O Skye,
Dearest of islands
(Alexander Nicolson)

Terry Marsh

CICERONE PRESS
MILNTHORPE, CUMBRIA

This book is dedicated to Margaret MacKenzie, my Skye landlady over many years.

ISBN 1 85284 220 2
First printed 1996, reprinted 1997
A catalogue record for this book is available from the British Library.

ACKNOWLEDGEMENTS

I am most grateful to Colin Paterson of Caledonian MacBrayne for complimentary passage between Mallaig and Armadale, and, for the supply and use of equipment and clothing, to Dave Brown of DB Mountain Sports (Kendal, England), and to Lowe Alpine (Tullamore, Ireland). Paul Franklin and Steve Yeates of Ordnance Survey very generously provided me with maps of Skye, from which I gleaned much vital information, and graciously listened to my advice about mapping needs on Skye. Colleagues in the Outdoor Writers' Guild have also been generous with their assistance: Rennie McOwan, for advice on access in Scotland; Kevin Walker, for permission to use extracts from his book *Safety on the Hills*; and Alan Hall, for help when my memory was floundering.

Gerry Ackroyd, Team Leader of the Skye Mountain Rescue Association, and proprietor of Cuillin Guides in Glen Brittle, read all of the walks text for me, and gave highly-valued advice and suggestions, all of which I used.

Paul and Grace Yoxon gave me permission to use their excellent booklets on the geology and prehistory of Skye as a basis for my own view of things.

I am much indebted to the many landowners and estate people on Skye who freely gave much assistance and advice, and, without exception, wished the book well.

But I could not conclude without acknowledging the cheerful humanity and unabated kindness that flowed from Mrs MacKenzie, to whom this book is dedicated, my landlady on Skye since I first discovered Caberfeidh, 2 Heatherfield, by Portree. Her gargantuan breakfasts and late evening 'tea and biscuits' have not only sustained me through many a visit, but, on occasion, proved more than I could lift through 3000 feet of ascent — it was then that I discovered Skye's coastal walking!

CONTENTS

Loch Scavaig to Loch Brittle

The Cuillin

[..] *indicates that the walk cannot be completed at all or in part without scrambling ability, as a minimum.*

Advice to Readers

Readers are advised that whilst every effort is taken by the author to ensure the accuracy of the guidebook, changes can occur which may affect the contents. It is advisable to check locally on transport, accommodation, shops, etc., while paths can be affected by forestry work, landslip or changes of ownership.

The publisher would welcome notes of any such changes.

This book has been compiled in accordance with the *Guidelines for Writers of Path Guides* published by the Outdoor Writers' Guild.

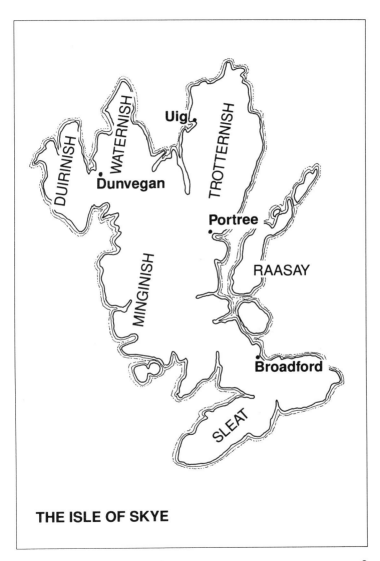

DUIRINISH
WATERNISH
Uig
TROTTERNISH
Dunvegan
Portree
MINGINISH
RAASAY
Broadford
SLEAT

THE ISLE OF SKYE

PREFACE

Thirty years ago, youthful and blissfully receptive to a new world of exploration that was only then opening up for me, I first set foot on Skye. An uncomfortable night in the car on the edge of Camas na Sgianadin gazing out to the island of Scalpay did nothing to diminish an enthusiasm to explore this remarkable island that has been sustained through all the following years. This was a vision of the Promised Land, full of hope and endless opportunities, a place of raw elemental forces, a land barely scratched by man.

On that first, exciting visit I travelled northwards through Portree and around Trotternish, round to Uig and out to Dunvegan, all on narrow, serpentine roads the remains of which you can still see beside the carriageways of modern-day Skye, bringing back happy memories every time I travel them. Bracadale, Glen Brittle, the Cuillin, the Elgol peninsula and Sleat, all were crammed into that hurried, mesmeric journey of discovery; it was a journey I have been making ever since, year on year, sometimes many times a year, and still, with the remarkable virtuosity for which Skye is famous among those who have fallen under its spell, I discover new nooks and crannies, odd corners never found before. It seems it will never end.

There is no compromise with Skye; you either love it or hate it, but, if you are still making up your mind, be advised, persistence does pay off. Tales of outrageous weather, days and days of a rain-lashed island, blasted furiously by winds that are as strong as any in Britain, are grossly exaggerated − true, but exaggerated. Come to Skye expecting and equipped for wind, rain and cold, and anything else is a bonus. But what a bonus! Yet to truly appreciate the charm of Skye you must see it in all its moods, and you must accommodate those moods, leaning on the wind, walking through the rain, and your reward will be bright, clear days, of vibrant colours, of seemingly infinite interest, way beyond your wildest imagination. And you must be patient.

But the weather is only one influence on the remarkable persona of Skye. Its geology and land forms are so diverse that the student of morphology and the landscape will find endless days of wonder here, while around its tortuous coastline the ubiquitous seas have taken their toll, and fashioned their own contribution to the Island's

grandeur. The Island's history is a microcosmos of human enterprise and endeavour, of resilience and mutual reliance on one's neighbours and fellow men.

Yet overriding everything, there hangs an indefinable, almost
supernatural quality that breeds a deep and abiding affection among
all those privileged to share Skye's secrets. Some describe it as 'the
Magic of Skye', Seton Gordon called it the 'Charm of Skye', others
'Skye fever'. Perhaps it has something to do with the elfin lore that
pervades this island of mist, or the invigorating purity of the air, or
the clarity of its light, or the wealth of legend, or simply the indelible
imprint Skye makes on an open and receptive mind.

Your passage and presence across the Skye landscape, a long-
established feature of access in Scotland generally, is matched by a
kindness and understanding from those who own the land, and those
who use it to produce a living. Proper and responsible appreciation
of that kindness and understanding will not go unrewarded.

To everyone who ventures on to Skye in search of the rewards I
have found, I wish you well and many hours of enjoyment that I know
will flow from your quest. Maintain your faith with Skye, and Skye
will keep its faith with you.

EXPLANATORY NOTES

Walking on Skye ranges from simple, brief outings not far from
civilisation, to rugged, hard mountain walking — as tough as any in
Britain — in isolated locations, where help is far away. Almost all of
it demands a good level of fitness and knowledge of the techniques
and requirements necessary to travel safely in wild countryside in
very changeable weather conditions, including the ability to use map
and compass properly [but note that the magnetic property of the
rock in the Cuillin makes the compass unreliable].

The walks in this book are widely varied in character and will
provide something for everyone, embracing high mountains, lonely
lochs, coastal cliffs and forests. Many walks visit places that are less
well known, where self-sufficiency is as important as it is among the
Cuillin.

But every walk is just that, a walk, and does not require rock
climbing or scrambling skills beyond the most fundamental. Even
so, the 'walker' must be fit and experienced enough to accomplish

ascents of the more accessible Munros and high peaks on the Island, ascents which though classed as 'walks' remain arduous and demanding undertakings. The point of division can best be explained as the moment when hands cease to be used simply for balance and security, and become necessary as an aid to progress. On this basis, Inaccessible Pinnacle remains inaccessible, but Sgurr Alasdair, the highest summit of the Cuillin, is included, in spite of the latter's toilsome scree slope and airy situation.

Where a walk is substantially available to non-scramblers, the route is described up to the difficulties. For example, the ascent of Sgurr nan Gillean is described as far as the topmost hundred feet or so; beyond that point the walker enters the realms of the hard scrambler. When a walk is substantially one that only competent scramblers or rock climbers could realistically attempt, no more than a brief description is given in the text, and the walk clearly identified as not suitable for walkers.

All parts of the Island, where walking is worthwhile, are visited, and the chosen walks will provide an excuse for many visits to the Island, and allow walkers to evade inclement weather in one part of the Island by seeking walks in another.

Each walk description begins with a short introduction, and provides Start and Finish points, as well as a calculation of the distance and ascent. The walks are grouped largely within the traditional areas of Skye, and, within those areas, in a reasonably logical order — allowance should be made, however, for the author's idiosyncratic brand of logic!

Distances:

Distances are given in kilometres (and miles), and represent the total distance for the described walk, i.e. from the starting point back to the finishing point. Where a walk continues from a previously-described walk, the distance given is the total additional distance involved. When a walk is to a single summit, the distance assumes a retreat by the outward route.

Ascent:

The figures given for ascent represent the total height gain for the complete walk, including the return journey, where appropriate. They are given in metres (and feet, nominally rounded up or down). Where a walk continues from a previously-described walk, the ascent figure is the total additional height gain involved.

This combination of distance and ascent should permit each walker to calculate roughly how long each walk will take using whatever method — Naismith's or other — you find works for you. On Skye, however, generous allowance must be made on most walks for the ruggedness of the terrain and the possibility that any streams that need to be crossed may prove awkward, or indeed completely impassable at the most convenient spot, necessitating long detours.

Access:

Within the author's knowledge there is and has been no problem of access on any of the walks in this book, but that does not mean that visitors should disregard crops, walls, fences, water supplies and buildings. Nor is there any suggestion that any of the routes included in this book forms a right of way.

In recent times, there has been a growing concern among sheep farmers about the presence of dogs. With increasing frequency you will encounter notices that ask you to keep your dog on a lead, and, in some cases, prohibit dogs. In the latter case, there is always a very good reason for doing so, usually because the walk covers ground close by sea cliffs that is grazed by free-roaming sheep, and over which startled sheep might fall. It is advisable to keep your dog on a lead at all times.

Safety:

The fundamentals of safety in the hills should be known by everyone heading for Skye intent on walking, but no apology is made for reiterating some basic do's and don'ts:

- Always take the basic minimum kit with you: Sturdy boots, warm, windproof clothing, waterproofs (including overtrousers), hat or balaclava, gloves or mittens, spare clothing, maps, compass, whistle, survival bag, emergency rations, first aid kit, food and drink for the day, all carried in a suitable rucksack.
- Let someone know where you are going.

- Learn to use a map and compass effectively.
- Make sure you know how to get a local weather forecast.
- Know basic first aid — your knowledge could save a life.
- Plan your route according to your ability, and be honest about your ability and expertise.
- Never be afraid to turn back.
- Be aware of your surroundings — keep an eye on the weather, your companions, and other people.
- Take extra care during descent.
- Be winter-wise — snow lingers in the Cuillin corries well into summer. If snow lies across or near your intended route, take an ice axe (and the knowledge to use it properly).
- Have some idea of emergency procedures. As a minimum you should know how to call out a mountain rescue team, and, from any point in your walk, know the quickest way to a telephone. You should also know something of the causes, treatment and ways of avoiding mountain hypothermia.
- Respect the mountain environment — Be conservation minded.

Maps:
1:50000: All the walks in this book can be found on Ordnance Survey® Landranger Sheets 23: North Skye; Sheet 32: South Skye; or Sheet 33: Loch Alsh, Glen Shiel and surrounding area.

1:25000: In addition Ordnance Survey produces an Outdoor Leisure Map (1:25000) Sheet 8: The Cuillin and Torridon Hills. To cover the whole island at a scale of 1:25000 you will currently need the OLM and at least 15 Pathfinder maps. Ordnance Survey, however, is constantly revising its publications and, at the time of writing, is looking at the possibility of producing more comprehensive maps for the island, at a scale of 1:25000.

Paths:
Not all the paths mentioned in the text appear on maps. Where they do, there is no guarantee that they still exist, remain continuous or well defined.

A number of the walks go close to the top of dangerous cliffs, both coastal and inland. Here the greatest care is required, especially in windy conditions. Do not, for any reason, venture close to cliff tops. Some of the routes rely on sheep tracks, which make useful paths in otherwise trackless areas. Sheep, however, do not appear to suffer from vertigo, and don't travel about with awkward, laden sacks on their backs. If a track goes towards a cliff, avoid it, and find a safer, more distant, alternative. Burns should be crossed at the most suitable (and safest) point; they can involve lengthy, and higher, detours in spate conditions. Do not allow the frustrations of such a detour to propel you into attempting a lower crossing against your better judgement.

If there are children in your party, keep them under close supervision and control at all times.

With only a small number of exceptions, paths are not waymarked or signposted. Many of the mountain paths, however, are cairned.

In a constantly developing environment like Skye, changes often occur to routes, especially through forests, or on coastal walks (as a result of landslip, for example). Notification of any such changes would be appreciated, via the publisher.

Language:

It is one of the continuing delights of Skye that you can still hear people speaking their native tongue, Gaelic (pronounced with a hard 'a', not 'ay'), and schools on the Island are giving bilingual classes in an endeavour to preserve the language.

And while the non-Gaelic-speaking visitor will find their first encounters with pronunciation a confusing and tongue-twisting experience, understanding, however, is not. The glossary of Gaelic words at the end of the book goes some way to helping with the translation. With only a little persistence, or a polite enquiry of a local, you can quickly gain sufficient mastery to render a good attempt at many of the more complex place-names.

To help with this understanding you will find a number of Gaelic dictionaries are available, along with books intended to assist you in coming to terms with this ancient language.

VISITOR INFORMATION

HOW TO GET THERE
The following information should be checked before finalising your travel arrangements.

BY ROAD
Access to the Island by road, without having to resort to ferries, became possible late in 1995 with the opening of the toll bridge from Kyle of Lochalsh to Kyleakin.

CAR FERRIES
There are two car ferry services from the mainland: Mallaig-Armadale is operated by Caledonian MacBrayne Limited, and Glenelg-Kylerhea is privately owned.

Mallaig-Armadale
The road journey from Fort William to Mallaig is one of the most scenic ways of approaching the Island; it is matched by an equally beautiful rail journey.
Contact: Mallaig: (01687) 462403, or Armadale (01471) 844248.
Crossing time: 30 minutes. Vehicle reservations required.
Operates Mondays to Saturdays (and Sundays 14 May-24 September): Up to 7 crossings daily (5 on Sundays).

Glenelg-Kylerhea
Approached over Mam Ratagan from Glen Shiel, the subsequent journey to the main Skye road climbs through the rugged Kylerhea Glen, a single track road with passing places and a very steep incline.
Contact: (01599) 511302.
Crossing time: 5 minutes. No reservations required.
Operates Maundy Thursday to mid-October: Mondays to Saturdays: 0900-1800 (June-September: 0900-2000), Sundays (from end of May-October only) 1000-1800.

BY RAIL
The Island is accessible by rail passengers from the south, via Glasgow (Queen Street) and Fort William-Mallaig (not Sundays). The 0812 train from Glasgow links with the 1200 train from Fort

William, to coincide with the 1345 car ferry.

An overnight sleeper service (The West Highlander) operates from London Euston to Fort William and Inverness, stopping at a number of intermediate stations.

Frequent daily services run from Glasgow and Edinburgh to Fort William for the Mallaig connection, and to Inverness for the service to Kyle of Lochalsh.

Contacts: All rail enquiries: 0345 212282.

BY AIR

There is a small airport on the Island, near Broadford, but no scheduled flights.

USEFUL INFORMATION AND ADDRESSES

The information given here may be subject to change from time to time, and should therefore be verified before travelling.

General:

Portree is the main town on the Island, with a full range of shopping facilities; Broadford also has a good range of facilities.

Accommodation:

The range of accommodation on Skye is extensive, including simple bunkhouses, bed and breakfast, guest houses and high quality hotels. The Tourist Information Offices will help you with finding accommodation, or you can consult the annual Skye Directory, available from tourist offices. The holiday guide *The Visitor*, is available free at tourist offices and elsewhere.

Tourist Information Offices:

Portree: (01478) 612137
Broadford: (May-September) (01471) 822361/822463

Banks:

Portree:
Royal Bank of Scotland (01478) 612822
Clydesdale Bank (01478) 612050
Bank of Scotland (01478) 612338
Broadford:
Bank of Scotland (01471) 822211

Bus Services:
— see timetables at Tourist Information Offices
Highland Bus and Coach Services: (01463) 233371
Portree-Broadford-Kyleakin-Armadale
Nicolson's Buses: (01470) 532240
Portree-Dunvegan-Staffin-Flodigarry-Uig-Kilmaluag-Storr-Glen Dale
Sutherlands Buses: (01478) 640400
Portree-Carbost-Glen Brittle-Portnalong-Fiscavaig
Skyeways Buses: (01599) 534328
Kyleakin-Portree-Broadford-Uig-Armadale

Post Bus:
Broadford-Elgol
Dunvegan-Glen Dale
Dunvegan-Waternish

Camping and Caravan Sites:
Dunvegan: Dunvegan Caravan Site, Dunvegan IV55 8WF
(01470) 521206.
Edinbane: Loch Greshornish Caravan and Camping Site, Edinbane,
Arnisort, by Portree IV51 9PS (01470) 582230.
Glen Brittle: Glenbrittle Farm IV47 8TA (01478) 640404.
Portree: Torvaig Caravan and Camping Site, Portree IV519HS
(01478) 612209.
Sligachan: Sligachan Campsite, Sligachan IV47 8SN
(01478) 650303.
Staffin: Staffin Caravan and Camping Site, Staffin IV51 9JX
(01470) 562213.
Uig: Uig Caravan and Camping Site, Uig IV51 9XU
(01470) 542360.

Car Repairs/Breakdown:
Portree: Ewen MacRae Ltd. (01478) 612554
Broadford: Sutherlands Garage (01471) 822225

Dentists:
Portree: (01478) 612582
Broadford: (01471) 822088

Doctors:
Ardvasar: (01471) 844283
Broadford: (01471) 822460
Borve: (01851) 850282
Carbost: (01478) 640202
Portree: (01478) 612013/612109

Hospitals:
Portree: (01478) 613200
Broadford: (01471) 822491

Mountain Guides:
Cuillin Guides, Stac Lee, Glen Brittle IV47 8TA (01478) 640 289

Mountain Rescue:
Alert Mountain Rescue Team at Portree Police Station on (01478) 612888

Petrol:
Armadale; Broadford; Dunvegan; Kyleakin; Portree; Staffin and Uig (NOTE: Only Broadford and Kyleakin petrol stations are open on Sundays throughout the year. Portree and Dunvegan stations are open on Sundays during the summer months.)

Police:
Portree: (01478) 612888

Youth Hostels:
Scottish Youth Hostels Association, 7 Glebe Crescent, Stirling, FK8 2JA (01786) 451181.

Armadale: Ardvasar, Sleat IV45 8RS (01471) 844260
Broadford: IV49 9AA (014718) 822442
Glen Brittle: Glen Brittle, Carbost IV47 8TA (01478) 640278
Kyleakin: IV41 8PL (01599) 534585
Uig: Uig, Portree IV51 9YD (01470) 542211

INTRODUCTION

Lovest thou mountains great,
Peaks to the clouds that soar,
Corrie and fell where eagles dwell,
And cataracts dash evermore?
Lovest thou green grassy glades,
By the sunshine sweetly kist,
Murmuring waves and echoing caves?
Then go to the Isle of Mist!

Described by the then Duke of York (later King George VI) during a visit in 1933, as "the isle of kind and loyal hearts", Eilean a'Cheo, the Isle of Mist, is second in size only to the Isle of Lewis in the Outer Hebrides It is known also as An t-Eilean Sgiathanach, the Winged Isle, because it can be viewed as a mighty bird with outstretched pinions, coming in to land, or to seize upon prey. Such has been the influence of Skye on the senses of visitors since the first tourists came to the Island that it has also assumed other names, all equally valid: The Isle of Enchantment, the Isle of Mystery, the Isle of Fantasy. To the Islanders, it is simply the Island, with a capital 'I', one of many islands, but to those for whom the Island is home, there is no comparison, no equal, no thought even that there might be.

By raven, Skye extends 78km (49 miles) from Rubha Hunish to the Point of Sleat, and if you travelled in a straight line overland from east to west you would cover 43km (27 miles). Yet such is the irregularity of the Island's coastline, probed by many fjord-like lochs, that you are rarely far from the sea, and never more than 8km (5 miles).

One of the earliest descriptions of Skye appeared in 1549, when Dean Munro wrote: "The iyle is callit by the Erishe, Ellan Skyane, that is to say in English, the Wingitt ile, be reason it has maney wings and points lyand furth frae it through the devyding of thir lochs."

The original derivation of the Island's name is lost, but many hold that it comes from 'Sgiath', the Norwegian for 'wing', while others contend it derives from another Norwegian word 'ski', meaning a mist, hence 'The Misty Isle'.

Setting aside these fundamental controversies of nomenclature, which merely serve to spark the flame of Skye's inordinate appeal, the Island is the most popular of all islands among tourists, mountaineers and walkers: botanists, photographers, natural history observers, too, find endless fascination within the bounds of Skye's ragged coastline.

Visiting walkers inevitably head for the Cuillin, unquestionably the most magnificent mountain group in Britain, yet there is so much more to Skye, and walking places, coastal and inland, are a perfect balance to the weight of the Cuillin. The most obvious of all the mountains on the Island are the Red Hills since the main road across the Island skirts around them. Once these are passed, however, you come into view of the Cuillin, a stark, jagged skyline that boldly impresses itself on the memory, yet when the cloud is down, they can be missed altogether.

The Island can be compartmentalised, if such is your desire, into districts. Most southerly is Sleat, though this is strictly an old parish name. Sleat abuts Strath, which extends northwards and west to the major promontories of the Island — Minginish (which embraces the Cuillin), Duirinish, Waternish and Trotternish. The 'nish' ending is of Norse derivation, and means promontory.

The Red Hills and the Cuillin Outliers lie within Strath, and more specifically a smaller promontory, owned by the John Muir Trust, Strathaird. Beyond the Cuillin and the Red Hills the highest peaks are close to Kyleakin, overlooking the mainland, while the most impressive form the long ridge of Trotternish. Elsewhere, abundant walking opportunity exists in all the main headlands and around the magnificent coastline; indeed the walk around the Duirinish coastline has no equal in Britain. It is part of Skye's appeal that each of these districts provides walking markedly different from its neighbours, which in sum, and in its own way, is every bit as satisfying as the Cuillin.

Walkers who combine the pleasure of physical exercise with an interest in flora and fauna, or in the history, culture and folklore of island races, will simply be spoiled for choice; there is nowhere on the Island that does not reward one's attention. As the poet Sorley MacLean wrote: "…a jewel-like island, love of my people, delight of their eyes…".

HISTORY

The history of Skye is quite simply a fascinating and time-consuming interest, and is nowhere better explained than in the immense and awe-inspiring detail of Alexander Nicolson's *History of Skye*, of which a second edition appeared in 1994. That is the work to consult: what follows here is, by comparison, a mere crumb from the table of this absorbing topic.

Wherever you go on Skye you encounter, if you care to look for them, remains of structural relics, ruins of houses, forts, tombs, and so on. The Island is almost littered with chambered cairns, hillforts, duns, brochs, hut circles, souterrains and Pictish stones, all, virtually without exception, dotted along the Island's tortured coastline. These are all that remain to tell us about the history of man on Skye before the days of the written word, and many of them date back more than 6,000 years.

Imagine, if you will, the scene during the last Ice Age, when Skye lay buried beneath enormous sheets of ice that even then were shaping the landforms with which we later became familiar. As climatic conditions warmed, so the glaciers retreated, a gradual, grinding process than ended between 10,000 and 11,000 years ago. As the incredible weight of ice disappeared, so the land began to rise, and improve as tundral conditions gave way to woodland and mixed vegetation. These conditions suited Mesolithic Man, who moved northwards, and settled around the new coasts, and among the islands. Mesolithic Man does not yet have a proven presence on Skye, man only occurring here during Neolithic times, though carbon dating of finds on the nearby island of Rhum at 6,000BC indicates not only the oldest known inhabitants in Scotland, but the possibility that Mesolithic Man also found his way to Skye, and the evidence of his presence yet to be found, or already lost.

Unlike Mesolithic Man, who lived as hunter gatherers, and moved on in search of food, Neolithic Man preferred a more static existence, staying for longer periods in the same place. This will account for the far greater number of Neolithic artefacts found not only among the Inner Hebrides, but generally throughout Britain. Neolithic Man moved to Britain from Europe about 6,000 years ago (c.4,000BC), and brought stocks of cattle and sheep, sowing grain, and living a simple farming existence.

About 2,000 years later (i.e. c.2,000BC) the Beaker People appear on the scene, also moving to Britain from Europe, especially from sites along the Rhine. They are so named from their practice of making ornate pottery. There are two particularly fine examples of chambered cairns dating from this period, one at Cnocan nan Gobhar (GR.553173), and the other, reached from Glen Brittle, at Rubh' an Dùnain (Walk 3.18).

By 1,000BC the first hillforts started appearing on Skye, signifying a sometime state of conflict between the local inhabitants and intruders. For about 800 years, hillforts dominated the landscape, varying in size, and usually consisting of a wall around an arrangement of internal buildings. Given the ready availability of wood on Skye, it is more than likely that the wall would have had a fence on top. They were all located on high ground, giving good views, and probably served as a focal point to which people living in surroundings homesteads might have retreated in times of danger.

Gradually, however, the size of these fortifications reduced, and they began to be replaced by duns, and later, brochs. Quite why this reduction occurred is not clear, but it is likely that as tribes became smaller, so the need for large enclosures was less. The result was the 'dun', a fairly simple structure, quite often little more than a wall set across a promontory, while a 'broch' by comparison was a highly sophisticated drystone achievement. The best preserved of the brochs on Skye is Dun Beag, off the Struan road to Dunvegan at GR.339386, near Bracadale.

The need for these defensive settlements was probably generated by invasions from mainland tribes. When these became preoccupied with the Roman presence further south, the result seems to have been a much more settled period of existence on Skye, and many of the brochs were abandoned, or robbed of their stone for the hut circles and souterrains that were to follow.

Hut circles were simply a ring of boulders on which a wooden structure was then built, and formed the basic homestead for farming communities. Souterrains, however, pose more of a problem, and probably served as underground defensive structures against the malice of cattle raiders. One of the best on Skye is at Claigan (GR.238539), north of Dunvegan.

There is little left on Skye of the so-called 'Pictish' era except a few standing stones, some bearing Christian-type crosses. A good example is at Clach Ard, 8km (5 miles) north-west of Portree, and bears rod symbols, and those for a mirror and a comb.

Subsequent to these times the Christian way of life began to take a strong hold, reinforced by the visit of St Columba in AD585, and other saints shortly after. But this period of calm was ended after a spell of only 200 years with the arrival of Viking invaders, and a new way of life.

The Norse occupation of the Island lasted until the Battle of Largs when the fleet of King Haco was defeated by the Scottish king Alexander III in 1263. Following this, the Western Isles were seceded to Scotland by the Treaty of Perth in 1266.

Yet, with a great independence of spirit for which the Islanders are renowned, they still saw themselves as separate from Scotland, led by the Lord of the Isles. Under his guidance there were many rebellions against the crown, especially during the fourteenth and fifteenth centuries, a period also noted for numerous feuds between the island clans. Of these the most prominent were the MacLeods and the MacDonalds, and the Island is spattered with sites of their deeds and misdeeds.

The position of Lord of the Isles was finally abolished by James IV in 1493, though this had little restraining impact on the clan chiefs in spite of a show of muscle by James V in 1540 who brought a large fleet to Skye, visiting the MacLeod and MacDonald strongholds at Dunvegan and Duntulm respectively before anchoring in Portree Bay while the chiefs came to pay their respects. Peace, of a sort, did then ensue, but only until the king died, and that but two years later. Clan battles continued to be waged throughout the sixteenth century, and just into the seventeenth, when the last battle, that in Coire na Creiche, was fought in 1601.

As one problem passed, so another appeared. During the seventeenth and eighteenth centuries life among the islands was coloured by attempts to restore the Stuarts to the throne of England and Scotland, the act of Union having taken place in 1603, when James VI of Scotland became James I of England on the death of Elizabeth I. These events came to a conclusion in the 1745 Rebellion led by Bonnie Prince Charlie (Prince Charles Edward Stuart) who, after his disastrous defeat at Culloden (1746) sought refuge in France by a most roundabout route that took him to the Outer Isles and to Skye itself, before leaving for the Scottish mainland and France in July 1746.

The 1745 Rebellion raised in Parliament the determination to completely erase the culture that had inspired the rebellion, and outlawed weapons, the Gaelic language and the wearing of the kilt. The attempt was successful, and peace came to the Islands.

But it was not to last. Poor harvests in 1835 and 1836 and a complete failure of the potato crop in 1846 and 1847 were circumstances that impoverished both the local population and their landlords, and led to a widespread clearance of the land so that the small crofts might be combined to form more profitable areas for sheep grazing. Landlords saw crofters as a burden rather than a means of income, and had little compunction in turning to the more viable sheep farming. Most of these forced evictions occurred between 1840 and 1885, when almost 7,000 families were moved from their land and sent abroad, many to die en route. Throughout this book, tales of these clearances appear again and again, and a number of walks visit the sites of former villages. It is a very emotive subject, and I doubt that anyone is proud of what happened, not even those who catalogue it as economic necessity. Towards the end of the nineteenth century people started resisting evictions and the tyranny that would often accompany them. Of key importance was a battle between crofters and police at Braes, not far from Portree, which led to a commission of inquiry and a number of successive crofters' laws which enshrined a security of tenure and fair rents, the substance of which remains intact today.

Agriculture still remains a major industry on Skye, but its future seems more likely to be founded on tourism, an economy set in being by the early attentions of Thomas Pennant, Johnson and Boswell, and Sir Walter Scott who visited Skye on his tour of the northern lighthouses in 1814. At the same time the first 'mountaineers' turned their attentions to the Island, concentrating almost exclusively, but with immense success, on the Cuillin. Once the single greatest range of mountain peaks in Britain became common knowledge, tourism gained a momentum it has never lost.

GEOLOGY

Almost certainly it was the geology of Skye that brought you to the Island. Not the study of geology, of course (though you may have come for that reason), but the consequences of the processes of tectonic creation that fashioned the profile and landscape of Skye.

Man has probably inhabited Skye for at least 4,000 years, but that is a brief moment of Skye's history, a history shaped over unimaginable years with many tools, the workings of which were at times cataclysmically violent, at others well-nigh undetectable.

As with the rest of Britain and Europe, the geological history of Skye dips back to the Pre-Cambrian era of about 2,500-3,000 million years ago, though millions of years would elapse before Skye became an island. Quite what the landscape was like in those distant times is only guesswork, but on the basis of geological and topographical studies Skye can be divided into three distinct sections.

First, the southernmost part of the island, Sleat, is composed of Lewisian Gneiss, Torridonian sedimentary rocks, Moine Schists and Cambro-Ordovician sedimentary rocks. The already complex interrelationships of these basic rock types is further complicated by extensive thrusting and the transportation of large areas of all these rocks. The present landforms are the product of massive glaciation which over most of the island flowed westwards, but along the east coast flowed northwards.

North Skye, including Trotternish, Waternish and Duirinish, consists of a plateau-like topography punctuated by sea lochs, as at Snizort, Dunvegan and Bracadale. Here, Jurassic sedimentary rocks occur, capped by lavas and pyroclastic rocks from the Lower Tertiary period. Because these rocks dip at a shallow angle to the west, they give rise to steep scarp slopes on the east side, and it is quite easy to pick out the different and distinctive lava layers. One spectacular feature of these rocks is the incidence of landslipped material which developed during Quaternary times; the Storr and the Quiraing are by far the best examples.

The most dramatic scenery, however, is formed from Lower Tertiary intrusive rocks, of which gabbro and granite are the most significant. It is from these rocks that the Cuillin are formed, and the distinction between these rocks and the intrusive acid rocks of the Red Hills is most noticeable as you walk through Glen Sligachan.

During the Tertiary period many parts of Skye were subjected to massive volcanic activity, probably the most violent in Britain. To the north-west of Kilchrist you can still see the vent of an ancient volcano; it has a diameter of about 5km (3 miles). When all that ceased, the island enjoyed about 50 million years of relative calm, until the ice came. The Pleistocene period, the Age of Ice, started about 2 million years ago, and is largely responsible for producing the landscape we see today. Massive ice sheets covered most of Britain, and huge glaciers flowed across the landscape, moving, plucking, breaking, scratching at the rocks below the ice. When finally they left, they had created a fascinating land form, one that was to be further shaped as sea levels fluctuated, forming raised beaches around Skye, and the agents of erosion got to work.

For a simplified study of these events you should read *The Geology of Skye*, by Paul and Grace Yoxon; for something vastly more in-depth you need *An Excursion Guide to the Geology of the Isle of Skye* by B R Bell and J W Harris.

FLORA AND FAUNA
In many respects the flora and fauna of Skye does not differ significantly from the rest of the Highlands and Islands of Scotland, but on a few counts the Island does stand out rather noticeably. Here you will find up to 40 percent of the world's grey seals, a high density of breeding golden eagles, and a more diverse flora and birdlife than any other comparable area in size in Europe.

And, of course, Skye boasts its own 'wee beastie' season. The midge is renowned worldwide, and can reduce the strongest of folk to tears. Sadly, this scourge of visitors from June to late summer has an accomplice, the cleg, a large horse-fly with a nasty bite. Proprietary defences are available in outdoor shops, and most work, up to a point, for a while. Scientists are currently working on developing midge-free areas, and on producing a repellent cream based on bog myrtle. A sprig of bog myrtle behind the ear is a traditional remedy of dubious success, while a dab or two of Oil of Lavender has been known to keep the midges at bay for a while, and raise an eyebrow or two if you forget to wash it off again before going into a confined public place, like a bar! Thankfully, midges hate wind, cold and heavy rain, and they should not normally cause a problem on coastal walks or among the high mountains; the theory is that they opt for the easier pickings on campsites.

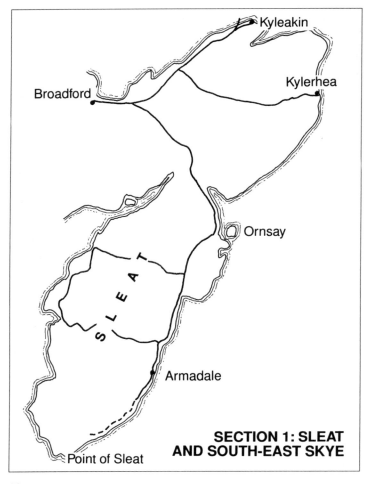

SECTION 1: SLEAT AND SOUTH-EAST SKYE

SECTION 1:
Sleat and South-east Skye

Sleat (pronounced slate) is the southernmost area of Skye, and projects from the main road between Kyleakin and Broadford near the township of Skulamus. To the north and north-east of this, in that convoluted way Skye has of making a nonsense of contrived partitioning, lies south-east Skye, and the closest point to mainland Scotland. It is here, in a region neither Sleat nor Strath, that you will find the only mountains of note. None is especially distinguished, but all provide excellent escapism from the summer clutter of the Cuillin, with the added bonus of outstanding panoramic views.

SLEAT

The name Sleat, derived from *sleibhte*, means an extensive tract of moorland, and so it is, an aptly-named thumb of rugged, rocky, lochan-laden moorland, creased into a thousand folds wherein man has fought with the elements to fashion a living. Yet Sleat is regarded as 'The Garden of Skye', though not without dissent, for to some extent the gardens are the product of an unhappy time in the Island's history, when clan chieftains succumbed to the rule of London, and rode roughshod over the lives and necessities of their tenants.

The appellation comes, too, from Sleat's more sheltered environment, protected from the worst of the Skye winds, that allows beech, sycamore and exotic conifers to flourish alongside the more natural birch, alder and bramble. Indeed, as Alastair Alpin MacGregor says: "It is at bramble-time that one should visit Russet Sleat of the beautiful women", a place once governed to a large extent by prosperous tacksmen who personally supervised the cultivation of their own particular farms. MacGregor records: "Slait is occupiet for the maist pairt be gentlemen, thairfor it payis but the auld deuteis, that is, of victuall, buttir, cheis, wyne, aill, and aquavite, samekle as thair maister may be able to spend being ane nicht...on ilk merkland. There is twa strenthie castells in Slait, the ane callit Castell Chammes, the uther Dunskeith".

The history of Sleat is essentially the history of the MacDonalds, in spite of legendary claims that it was the second-century Irish folk hero Cuchullin who came to Dunscaith to learn the art of war from Queen Sqathaich, and the fact that there was a time when all of Skye, including Sleat, was MacLeod territory. By 1498, Dunscaith was in MacDonald possession, and continued to be lived in until the early part of the seventeenth century.

For the walker there is in Sleat none of the rugged grandeur found further north on the Island, indeed much of the interior of Sleat will find greater favour with those more interested in natural and social history than walking. But if the walker comes in search of solitude or peaceful havens in which to reflect for a time, there can be no better place on Skye. Most walks, however, need no description, and little more effort than to park the car and wander about the moorland expanse, or seek out a sheltered nook along the coastline.

The main road, the A851, runs south as far as Armadale, beyond which a minor road makes a valiant, if vain, attempt to probe fully to the Point of Sleat. Many visitors come to Skye, as I did, via the ferry from Mallaig to Armadale, and so gain completely the wrong first impression of Skye. But if you come on to the Island (ideally) from Glenelg to Kylerhea, or Kyleakin via the new bridge, you receive a vastly different set of values with which to form your opinion, values more closely approximating the overall ambience of Skye.

With this rather different perspective, if you set off into Sleat from Skulamus, then you will gain immensely from the contrast, especially if you have already toured some of the Island first, for then it is that you absorb the differences that earned Sleat its gardenlike title; differences that give Sleat, in places, an 'English' flavour. As Otta Swire comments: "Trees abound...every house of any importance has its woods and lawns as in England. Rhododendrons are plentiful and in the spring the bluebells and primroses could vie with Kent. The road is bounded in many places with the type of hedgerow which one associates with Devon lanes, hedges of hawthorn, wild rose, and elder".

Yet there are many places where the 'feel' is truly that of Skye and the west of Scotland. From Skulamus you first encounter flat moorland and a landscape dotted with island-studded lochans, across which Loch Eishort is sure to catch your eye. It is only as you pass Duisdale, for several generations belonging to the MacKinnons for services as standard bearers to the MacDonalds of Sleat, that a noticeable change occurs. Near magical Isle Ornsay, the road heads away from the coast, and passes by Loch nan Dubhrachan, once inhabited by a monster (The Beast of the Little Horn).

Not far from the loch a minor road loops round to Ord, Dunscaith and Tarskavaig, a splendid drive with many opportunities to patrol the beaches on Sleat's northern coastline, gazing across Loch Eishort to the mountainous country beyond.

Armadale merely serves to underscore the 'southern' feel of Sleat, the castle, built in the eighteenth century, attractively set amid woods and lawns. There is some lack of certainty about when Armadale was built. One record claims it for Alexander Wentworth of Sleat, born in 1775; another, published in 1725, mentions a "place of residence, adorned with stately edifices, pleasant gardens and other policies called Armodel"; while yet earlier records detail, in 1690, how Armadale House was burned by the King's fleet.

Sleat does not end at Armadale. Beyond lies Ardvasar, quite a large township on Armadale Bay, and beyond that the scattering of buildings that comprise Aird of Sleat, the final gateway to southernmost Skye at the Point of Sleat.

SOUTH-EAST SKYE

With the opening of the new bridge between Kyle of Lochalsh and Kyleakin in 1995, the Island lost its total independence, and gained a speedier link between island and mainland, though only the summer months saw any significant delay. Quite what the effects will be only time will tell: perhaps the trade of both ports will diminish as motorists hasten by instead of stopping; maybe the tiny ferry that plies between Glenelg and Kylerhea will sink (hopefully not literally) under the weight of purists shunning the bridge in favour of traditional ways of reaching the Island; perhaps someone will devise a bridge to Kylerhea, and blaze a wide road up to the Bealach Udal and down Glen Arroch.

In this first foothold corner of Skye lie the highest summits outwith the Black and Red Cuillin. Just east of Kyleakin, on a small promontory, stands Castle Maol, sometimes referred to as Dun Akin. The main wall was massively damaged in a storm on 1 February 1948. The castle is claimed to have been the residence of a Norwegian princess, known as 'Saucy Mary', who may well have been the princess that lies buried on the summit of Beinn na Caillich.

Typically, this ancient ruin, the very first thing that used to be encountered as you crossed on to the Island, is a classic example of the quagmire one descends into the moment any inquiry is made into the fascinating history of Skye. Much of Skye's history is well documented, but the truth of Castle Maol is obscure. According to legend, the castle was built in the twelfth century by Mary, who is said to have devised a chain across the kyle from a point below the castle, by means of which she prevented foreign vessels from passing until they had paid a toll. One book, however, records: "The older part [of the castle] is thought to date back to the tenth century; while the newer portion is possibly early fifteenth". It was certainly there in 1513 when a meeting of clan chiefs met to raise Sir Donald MacDonald of Lochalsh to the status of Lord of the Isles. Jim Crumley (*The Heart of Skye*) claims that Beinn na Cailleach "marks the burial chamber of an eighth-century Norse princess who lived at Castle Maol". Seton Gordon (*The Charm of Skye*) plays safe, and only ventures to suggest that the princess "may have been the same proud ruler who dwelt in Caisteal Maol".

The truth is, it doesn't matter. No one knows for certain, yet so much intrigue and fascination flows from this one crumbling edifice, and sets a standard by which inquiring minds will clatter away over the myriad similar circumstances and queries that Skye has to offer, probably *ad infinitum*.

A short way round the coastline you reach the Sound of Sleat, and, at Kylerhea, the place where drovers used to cross thousands of cattle each year to the mainland at slack water, linked nose to tail, and the first tied to a rowing boat. It must have been a fascinating spectacle, the more so because, as Gavin Maxwell recounts in *A Ring of Bright Water*, the sound was visited from time to time each year by killer whales.

In the opposite direction you head around the coast to Broadford, through an area, still wooded, but formerly densely so, and part of an ancient Caledonian forest.

The hinterland of south-east Skye, between the A851 and the kyles, is wild, rugged and unforgiving, no place for noviciate exploration. With the benefit of experience, however, this rough terrain will

Bla Bheinn South Ride from the track to Camasunary
Crossing the river at Camasunary

Garsbheinn, Sgurr na Stri and Camasunary
Basteir Tooth and Sgurr a'Fionn Choire

provide hours of adventure, and stakes a worthy claim to the attention of all walkers who venture on to Skye.

WALK 1.1:
Gleann Meadhonach and Dalavil

Sleat is not renowned for an over-abundance of walking opportunity. Though possessing a fascinating coastline of rocky inlets and tiny beaches, the hinterland is a troubled landscape of heathery knolls and boggy, lochan-ridden moorland, punctuated sparsely by man's efforts to win a living from it. That he often fails is evidenced by the ruined crofts and agricultural buildings that dot the scene, though some, as along this walk through Gleann Meadhonach to secluded Dalavil, are as a result of clearances carried out on the Island during the nineteenth century.

> **Start/Finish:** Roadside lay-by on minor road to Achnacloich. GR.623067.
> **Distance:** 12km (7½miles).
> **Ascent:** 200m (655 feet) — mostly on the return journey.

From the minor road that links Kilbeg and Achnacloich walk south-west down from the road, keeping left of a telegraph pole and heading out across the moorland, aiming for a small rise ahead. Following sheep tracks, you cross a number of streams, and within a couple of miles pass the first signs of ruined habitations. By keeping to the highest of the sheep tracks progress will be somewhat easier, and shortly brings Loch a'Ghlinne and the sea beyond into view. The loch is a favoured haunt of wintering whooper swans.

The route continues, descending gently to a point where you can enter the woodland of Coille Dalavil. Here you will find a more substantial track, and as it emerges from the trees you can see, away to the left, the watercourse the former inhabitants of Dalavil constructed to drain the surrounding land and the loch: the loch itself is barely 6m (20 feet) above sea level, and much of the glen is frequently waterlogged.

An on-going path leads to the remains of Dalavil township, and in due course the sea. If you keep to the higher ground above Dalavil, you will experience a beautiful moment as the inlet of Inver Dalavil springs into view. To the north-west the Elgol peninsula is set against the bulk of the Red Cuillin, with the Black Cuillin rising starkly above the low island of Soay, once used as a base by Gavin Maxwell for a shark fishery, and recounted in his book *Harpoon at a Venture*. Out to sea, the Cuillin of Rhum stand darkly on the horizon, with the island of Eigg to their left.

When you have explored sufficiently, simply retrace your steps to the Achnacloich road.

Dalavil

As Jim Crumley points out in The Heart of Skye, *Dalavil, as you find it today is the product of a motive that bred "maximum profit and the minimum inconvenience for an accursed breed of morally corrupt landlords". Yet, unlike other cleared townships, such as Suisnish and Boreraig, Dalavil was cleared for an altogether different reason, at the time of the Education Acts of 1870-2. Writer David Craig* (On the Crofters' Trail), *records: "It was for the children to get their schooling. It was cheaper to clear the crofters than to build a school there. It was quite isolated – there was no road to it, just a path over the hill. It was a very good place for fishing, plenty of mackerel, and ling, and again there was shellfish too, and there was a lot of [sea]weed for their crops, for their potatoes and whatever they were turning".*

Here the families were mostly the MacKinnons, MacGillivrays and Robertsons. As their children grew they looked up at "the terraced black drop of Doire na h'Achlais where wild water sheds its veils and jets of spume and wondered, 'When will it stop? Why does it come in jerks instead of smoothly?'" – a charmingly naive view of life, that would speak volumes if focused on the irony of the latter-day slash of intrusive roadway, constructed to make it easier for estate vehicles to reach the loch, set against the very reason, i.e. the absence of a road, that denied the children of Dalavil a school.

WALK 1.2:
Acairseid an Rubha
and Point of Sleat

This expedition to the southernmost tip of Skye is unlikely to need more than a few hours away from home, but crams countless delights into that brief time-span, especially if you go there in spring and early summer when the fields are ablaze with colour, and the air loud with bird-song. The walk also visits the delightful inlet of Acairseid an Rubha, where many visitors conclude their outward walk.

The approach is along the road from Ardvasar to the Aird of Sleat, where parking is very limited and needs to be accomplished with consideration for others.

Start/Finish: Road end, near Aird old church. GR.589007.
Distance: 9km (5¾ miles).
Ascent: Nominal, spread over many undulations.

Beyond a gate follow a cart track over heather-clad moorland, with Rhum at one point suddenly putting in an appearance and a moment's pause providing a fine retrospective view. Descend and keep on along the path that follows, passing a house, crossing wooden plank bridges over the burn that flows from Loch Aruisg, and continuing through a gate to a sheltered inlet where there is a house and cottage. This is Acairseid an Rubha, a splendid place for exploration and relaxation.

To reach the Point of Sleat, return to the path and turn right (south), now keeping to the higher ground, though the route is not always obvious, and some of the intervening ground prone to bogginess. The general direction, however, is never in doubt, and no one is going to get seriously lost making for the Point. Over a stone slab spanning a burn climb a rock stairway continuing along the line of a fence. When you finally quit the fence, go half left (south-east) along a low ridge and ascend to a gap above Camas Daraich, where I have spent many a relaxed hour watching black-throated and great northern divers patrolling warily.

A better path now runs south-west across the moorland, crossing to the west of this neat peninsula. Go down steps to the inlet below and round the shore to a causeway by which you cross to the Point of Sleat. A short ascent of more steps leads past a hut to the light-house, and the most southerly point of Skye.

Just to the west of the Point, Eilean Sgorach is a favoured gathering ground for cormorants, where they stand drying outstretched wings. The view is dominated by the mainland, and the island of Rhum, but on a warm, settled day you could be a million miles from anywhere, resolving clouds, soaking in the gentlest of sea breezes, without a care in the world.

Your return journey can only be by the outward route.

WALK 1.3:
Sgurr na Coinnich

With its near neighbour, Beinn na Caillich, Sgurr na Coinnich lies in a rough corner of Skye, the first aspect of the island seen, other than at a distance, by visitors arriving via Kyle of Lochalsh. A better view is to be had from Glenelg, across the Sound of Sleat, and it is from this direction, by way of the Kylerhea ferry, that strong walkers might come to effect a quick sortie on the tussock grass and heather flanks of these craggy, infrequently-visited hills.

You can park at Kylerhea, cross the Sound as a pedestrian passenger, walk up Kylerhea Glen to Bealach Udal, tackle both summits from there, and return to Kylerhea by way of Beinn Bhuidhe; not a prospect for the faint-hearted, but a good and satisfying round that will require between 5 and 6 hours once on the island.

> **Start/Finish:** Bealach Udal. GR.753207. Limited parking.
> **Distance:** 4km (2¼miles).
> **Ascent:** 460m (1510 feet).

The untracked ascent from Bealach Udal is initially very rough and crag-ridden, but can be eased, slightly, by setting off from a little lower down Kylerhea Glen, from the point where the road starts to descend steeply towards Kylerhea. From here you can reach the south ridge, though it is not very prominent as such, by keeping to the left of a conspicuous buttress (due south of the small lochan at GR.760209, for which you should first navigate). Once round the buttress head for the south ridge and another, larger lochan at GR.759220, from where you can gain the summit ridge and so the top of the hill. As you climb, you leave much of the difficult terrain behind, moving rather more easily on short turf, that comes as a fine reward for the effort lower down.

The summit view is quite spectacular — a phrase that could be used for almost every mountain top on the Island — embracing the kyles at your feet, the mainland peaks, and the great thumb of the Sleat peninsula. The speediest return is by your outward route, though the ascent of Sgurr na Coinnich is usually combined with that of Beinn na Caillich (see Walk 1.4).

Kylerhea
Kylerhea is named after one of the Fiennes, who lived near Glenelg, Mac an Raeidhinn, who, racing back to his village, which was under attack, failed in his attempt to leap the Sound at this point.

The kyle is a valuable sanctuary for wildlife, especially otters, seals and the wide variety of seabirds that visit these coastal waters. Sharks, too, pass this way from time to time.

WALK 1.4:
Beinn na Caillich

Said to be named after Grainnhe, wife of Fionn, chief of the Fiennes, Beinn na Caillich has rather more shape to it than its sibling, Sgurr na Coinnich, and is both a worthy companion and a logical extension of the marginally higher summit. It lies 1km (½ mile) north-east of Sgurr na Coinnich across much the same awkward terrain.

Beneath Grainnhe's grave on the summit of the hill is reputed to lie a large crock filled with gold and jewels, for so great a lady was she that at her burial every man of the Fiennes cast their rarest jewels into an earthenware crock to do her honour.

> **Start/Finish:** Continues from Walk 1.3 Sgurr na Coinnich.
> **Additional distance:** 2km (1¼ miles).
> **Additional ascent:** 320m (1050 feet).

Between the two summits, the Bealach nam Mulachag, necessitates a descent and reascent in the order of 160m (525 feet), which needs repeating if you are returning to Bealach Udal. Although Beinn na Caillich is predominantly rocky, sufficient oases of grass appear to ease progress, best achieved in a north-east direction from the bealach. Take care on the return not to be drawn towards the hill's steep western face, which can be confusing in misty conditions.

The summit has unrivalled views of the hustle and bustle at Kyleakin and the Kyle of Lochalsh, and the new road bridge that links the Plock of Kyle, Eilean Bàn and Skye, above which it maintains a respectable distance.

Walkers retreating to Kylerhea should return to Bealach nam Mulachag, and then strike south-east over Beinn Bhuidhe. Those heading for Bealach Udal should simply retrace their steps.

WALK 1.5:
Ben Aslak

Ben Aslak rises on the south side of the Kylerhea Glen to which it presents a rugged northern face; the southern aspect, spilling down to the Sound of Sleat, is rather less interesting.

> **Start/Finish:** Bealach Udal. GR.753207. Limited parking.
> **Distance:** 4km (2½ miles).
> **Ascent:** 420m (1380 feet).

The easiest approach is from Bealach Udal, and involves first tackling a minor top, Beinn Bheag, reached across heathery, crag-punctuated slopes. Go south and south-east from this top to gain a narrow col, before ascending to a small lochan, and from there pulling up more heathery slopes, aiming slightly closer to south (right) as you approach the summit.

Ben Aslak has two summits about 400m (1300 feet) apart, the higher being that to the west. Both, however, are good viewpoints: the higher summit for views of the distant Cuillin, while the eastern top gives appetising glimpses into the rough mainland ground of Knoydart beyond Loch Hourn.

A determined soul could press on south-westwards with difficulty across Bealach na Cruinn-leum to include Beinn Dubh a'Bhealaich and Beinn na Seamraig, but with little reward for the effort, and a tiring return to Bealach Udal, or a weary moorland slog to reach Kinloch Lodge Hotel or the A851, to which transport would have to be arranged.

WALK 1.6:
Kylerhea Glen circuit

This tough and unremitting circuit of the wild and rugged Kylerhea Glen is no light undertaking, and should not be contemplated other than by experienced walkers, and only then in good conditions. Given those conditions, it is a superbly satisfying round, and one you will almost certainly have to yourself.

Start/Finish: Kylerhea slip. GR.788212.
Distance: 14km (8¾ miles).
Ascent: 1295m (4250 feet).

It begins with a direct assault on Beinn Bhuidhe, from there tracking below Sgurr na Coinnich to the Bealach nam Mulachag. From the bealach, ascend Beinn na Caillich, and return to climb Sgurr na Coinnich, before descending south-westwards to Bealach Udal on the Broadford-Kylerhea road. Now, cross the road and tackle the heathery slopes of Beinn Bheag, before pressing on to Ben Aslak.

Once the summit of Ben Aslak is gained, head for its eastern top, and from there descend the long and easily-inclined north-east ridge until you intersect the coastal path linking Kylerhea with Kinloch Lodge Hotel above Loch na Dal. Head north along this path to reach a bridge over Kylerhea River. Go ahead alongside a fence to reach an unsurfaced road near a house, and there turn right to follow the road out to the main glen road, not far from your starting point.

WALK 1.7:
Coastal path: from Loch na Dal to Kylerhea

The fine, but remote, coastal path linking Loch na Dal and Kylerhea is a magnificent escape for seekers of solitude, and though not an unduly long walk, is quite demanding, needs transport at either end and the ability to cope with any emergencies that might arise; in the middle stretches of the walk you are remarkably isolated from outside help. Backpackers touring the island on foot will find this a splendid, if roundabout, way of leaving the island.

The walk begins through Kinloch Forest, where there is indeed a fine circular forest walk that visits the site of Leitir Fura (Letterfura), a scattering of lonely homesteads finally vacated in 1782, of which very little now remains, or, for that matter, is recorded. During the eighteenth century, the natural woodland at Leitir Fura was by far the largest on the Island, though barely more than 5km (3 miles) in length. Today, Leitir Fura is the most westerly ashwood in the UK, and has some nationally important bryophytes and lichens. In recent times, many non-native species have been removed and ground opened up for natural regeneration to occur.

Throughout the walk you have the Sound of Sleat for company, the mainland hills that backdrop Glenelg, and the Sandaig Islands, made famous, as Camusfearna by Gavin Maxwell in A Ring of Bright Water. *Forestry Enterprise has plans to develop walks in the Kinloch Forest, and these may vary the route description given here, notably at the Kinloch end.*

Start: Roadside parking on A851, shortly after turning to Drumfearn. GR.693165.
Finish: Kylerhea.
Distance: 11½km (7 miles).
Ascent: 200m (655 feet).

From the roadside parking go along a forest road that soon crosses the Abhainn Ceann-locha, and continue to a junction where the road forks, one road leading, right, to the Kinloch Lodge Hotel. Ignore this branch, and go ahead on a broad track into woodland that has been designated as a Site of Special Scientific Interest (SSSI). Press on for 1km (½ mile), until just before a gate you can divert on to the Kylerhea Path, an old drove road that leads to the site of Leitir Fura. [Some of the most enlightening reading on the drove roads on Skye may be found in Haldane's *The Drove Roads of Scotland*, and a more recent publication *The Famous Highland Drove Walk* by Irvine Butterfield.]

The onward path, once you have explored Leitir Fura, is generally straightforward, but invariably wet in many places, and climbs quite high on to the south-eastern flanks of Beinn na Seamraig. The views are extensive throughout the walk, and present many mainland favourites from an unusual angle.

As you approach Kylerhea, the path crosses Kylerhea River by a bridge, and runs on alongside a fence and then right, beside the river, to an unsurfaced track linking Kylerhea village with the glen road.

WALK 1.8:
Kylerhea Trail

This very easy walk is one on which essential equipment includes a pair of binoculars as it visits a viewing hide overlooking a stretch of the kyle much favoured by otters, seals and seabirds. Don't expect a ready display of these beautiful creatures, but patience mingled with fortune will provide a memory of Skye that is second to none.

The start of the walk is found not far from the Kylerhea ferry slip, at the far end of Kylerhea Glen, reached by a narrow and circuitous round through a fascinating landscape from the main Kyleakin — Broadford road, near the airstrip.

> **Start/Finish:** Car park. GR.787212. Please note: Dogs are not allowed on this trail; the scent of a dog can disturb the wildlife of the area.
> **Distance:** 4½km (3 miles)(maximum).
> **Ascent:** Negligible.

Leave the car park, following the broad trail, and soon pass through a gate giving access to the nature reserve. There are throughout the walk good views across the kyle to the wooded slopes of Druim na Leitire, and of the habitat customarily frequented by otters, in particular.

As you approach the viewing hide, do keep noise to a minimum, otherwise any chance of seeing otters and the many other species of wildlife that frequent this coast will vanish.

The hide is usually manned by staff of Forest Enterprise, and they will give advice about what to look for, as will the displays within the hide.

As you leave the hide, turn right down a wooded trail for a short detour, past a miniature waterfall and pool, to climb steps back on to the main trail. Turn right, and follow the trail, either as far as you like or until it ends, close by the power lines overhead. Any thoughts of pressing on through the forest should be banished. The path does continue a short way, but becomes impenetrable before long.

Simply go back to the car park along the main trail, scanning the slopes of Beinn Bhuidhe for a glimpse of deer or a golden eagle.

Otters

Otters are members of the Mustelidae family, which includes weasel, stoat and mink, and an average sized otter will measure about 1.2m (4 feet). They will eat anything, and have a hearty appetite, though their main diet comprises fish, crustaceans, amphibians and small mammals.

Otters are a protected species under the Wildlife and Countryside Act 1981, under the provisions of which it is an offence

*intentionally to disturb an otter in its place of shelter, or knowingly
to approach its holt.*

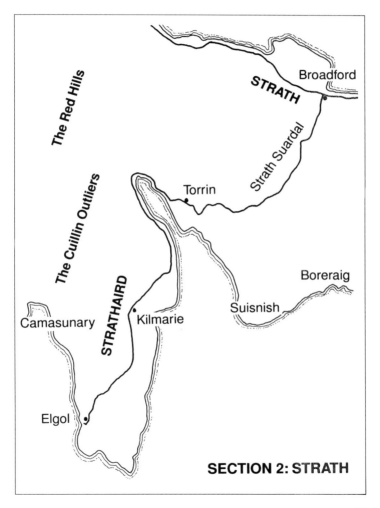

SECTION 2:
Strath

If you were to search for one area of Skye that contains a taste of everything you might find elsewhere, you need look no further than Strath. It is a unique area, with an unusual independence, neither North Skye nor South Skye, neither MacLeod territory nor MacDonald. This was MacKinnon country, sandwiched between the two frequently warring factions, and adept at keeping the peace with both — which is probably why the MacKinnons earned the uncomplimentary nickname 'Two-Faced'.

Bounded on the north by Loch Sligachan and the south by Lochs Scavaig, Slapin and Eishort, Strath extends westwards from Broadford Bay as far as Glen Sligachan. Within this loch-probed sanctuary lies some of the most fascinating and widely-varied walking ground on the Island, ranging from coastal exploration around the Strathaird peninsula and along the north shore of Loch Eishort, to the domed scree-heights of the Red Cuillin and the dark Cuillin Outliers, culminating in the single most attractive mountain on Skye, Bla Bheinn. Here there is something for everyone; nor will walkers less intent on conquering mountains than mere exploration be any less disappointed, for here there are ruined villages, stone circles, limestone caves, sandstone cliffs, prehistoric cairns, great glens, coastal geos, and a tremendous wealth of social and natural history.

Strath, too, seems to have been a major centre of religious importance since the earliest times, and there is evidence of both pagan and Christian religions throughout the entire region. Quite often you will find the remnants of both forms of religion almost side by side, ruined churches standing close by stone circles, a clear suggestion that although St Columba sought to convert the pagan people of Skye to Christianity he was not so foolhardy as to demolish their sacred places.

The key to much of the area is the seemingly innocuous road that sets off Elgol-bound from the town of Broadford. The road first enters lovely Strath Suardal beneath the red hills of Beinn na Caillich, Beinn Dearg Mhor and Beinn Dearg Bheag. It all seems now to be a place of peace, flowing richly with the enchantment of the wild, heavy with the charm of the past, but during the times of Creation, this same glen was the source of immense and violent volcanic upheaval. On the opposite side of Loch Cill Chriosd you can still see the site of the main vent, now filled with coarse-grained material.

As you journey down the road you encounter first, just at a bend, a green knoll that bears the name An Sithean. This means 'fairy hill', and here at night and with a receptive mind, you may well hear the sounds of fairy music rising through the ground. Whether or not you believe in fairies, An Sithean gives you a good view of Coire-chat-achan, the MacKinnon home twice visited by Johnson and Boswell during their visit to Skye in 1773, and a year earlier by Thomas Pennant.

Further into the glen and you reach the ruined church of Cill Chriosd, ivy- and cotoneaster-clad, surrounded by a graveyard much older than the church, and which may date from prehistoric times. The church, the former parish church of Strath, evidently existed in the early sixteenth century, and probably during the late fifteenth, but had ceased to be used by 1840, due to its state of disrepair.

On a clear day, Strath Suardal is a wonderful place of great beauty, but wreathed in mist, it assumes an eerie air, and favours well the claim that "The waste is haunted...by Ludag, a malignant goblin, that in the [eighteenth century] used to be seen at dusk hopping with immense hops on its one leg — for unlike every other denizen of the supernatural world, it is not furnished with two — and that, enveloped in rags, and with fierce misery in its hollow eye, has dealt heavy blows, it is said, on the cheeks of benighted travellers". Loch Cill Chriosd, too, is said to be haunted, by a terrible monster which laid waste to the land, and carried off and devoured women and children. Not until St Maelrhuba blessed the waters of the loch was the monster laid to rest, since when the loch waters are said to have held great healing powers.

Soon the glen runs out to the crofting township of Torrin, and on to reach the shores of Loch Slapin, beyond which towers the great grey, splintered bulk of Bla Bheinn, inspiration of many poems, and considered by Alexander Nicolson, local pioneer of Cuillin exploration, to be the finest hill on Skye. With so many fine summits in attendance, the discerning walker might spend a week or more among the hills and glens of Strath, without once adjourning to the Cuillin heights for satisfaction of his or her needs.

Then, at the end of Srath Mór, the Elgol road loops around the head of Loch Slapin, to meander down the Strathaird peninsula, from where Prince Charles Edward Stuart finally left Skye for mainland Scotland, and France.

Coastal walking, and the famous Spar Cave, await the visitor to southernmost Strathaird, while from the township of Elgol, the view across Loch Scavaig of the Cuillin is one of which Skye-lovers will never tire.

WALK 2.1:
Broadford Coast and forest walk

This uncomplicated walk occupies the wedge of land north of the A850-Portree road, and north-west of the town. Good paths start and finish the walk, though some of the intervening section is rough and pathless. The final return to Broadford is along what remains of the old narrow road by means of which I made my first, memorable excursions to Skye close on 30 years ago.

Start/Finish: Car park, Broadford. GR.643235.
Distance: 8km (5 miles).
Ascent: Nominal.

Leave the Broadford car park and turn right, heading towards Portree. After the bridge take the first turning on the right, and go down to the pier. On the way you pass the Broadford youth hostel, ideally placed for exploration of this fascinating region of Skye. Keep ahead through a gate, following the on-going road past Corry Lodge to reach the shore path at an iron gate.

Shortly, climb left to the top of the headland, Rubh' an Eireannaich (Irishman's Point). Cross a fence and go round the corner of a wall to follow the path through October-vibrant heather back to the shore, with fine views of the far mainland, and the more local islands — the

Crowlins, Pabay, Longay, Scalpay and Guillamon Island — for illustrious company.

When another fence is crossed (stile), rather more uncomfortable walking begins, where essentially you are left to your own devices, switching between the ubiquitous basaltic rocks of the shore and heather knolls above. Care is needed whenever you cross basalt, but especially if it is wet. Take your time as you move on as this is a place to relax and linger, and agreeably attractive in early summer when the wild flowers are at their best, or in the teeth of a Skye storm when progress is an exhilarating, breath-taking struggle against the elements.

You eventually rejoin the shore near a clearing, once occupied by man, as the remains of croft buildings testify. The difficult passage now relents as you pursue a path between woodland and the shore. At a bend, a small bay comes into view, leading on to Rubha na Sgianadin, where your attention will be caught by the great pile of Beinn na Caillich.

Amble around Camas Sgianadin, a pleasant bay, where you join a forest trail back to the main road, reaching the A850 near the cemetery. All that remains is to follow the old road back to Broadford, reflecting no doubt on the leisurely passage that would have prevailed only a few years ago, and the angry haste of modern-day travellers on the new autobahnstrasse, bound for Portree and the secrets of northern Skye.

WALK 2.2:
Coire Gorm Horseshoe

The three summits that form the Coire Gorm Horseshoe — Beinn na Caillich, Beinn Dearg Mhór and Beinn Dearg Bheag — lie to the west of Broadford, the highest of these, Beinn na Caillich, brooding above the town and capped by a huge cairn visible for miles. Beneath the cairn, it is said, lies a Norwegian princess, possibly the same one who dwelt at Caisteal Maol at Kyleakin and stretched a chain across the sound so that she could levy a toll on passing ships. When the princess lay dying, and knew that the end of her life was imminent, she asked that she might be buried, as Seton Gordon recounts in The Charm of Skye, "full in the track of the Black Wind that sweeps, pure, cold, and vital, across from the shores of Lochlin, hundreds of leagues beneath the pale northern horizon". Over her body, her compatriots erected a huge cairn, while beneath her body, so the story goes, lies a casket of gold.

The walk begins from near the remains of the MacKinnon household from where Thomas Pennant climbed Beinn na Caillich in 1772, thereby effecting the first recorded ascent of any summit on Skye. Johnson and Boswell stayed at Coire-chat-achan for two nights a year later, but appear to have been singularly unimpressed by the mountains of the Island.

Coire-chat-achan means the Corrie of the Wild Cats, and commemorates the last habitat of wild cats on Skye before their extermination. It is reached by taking a minor road on the left about 2 km (1 mile) along the A850-Portree road from Broadford. The road runs on past forest to a turning area where the tarmac ends. You can park here if you can do so without causing obstruction. The slopes of Beinn na Caillich rise above you, a seemingly impossible approach, and though indeed strenuous they are far less demanding than they appear.

Start/Finish: Coire-chat-achan. GR.619227.
Distance: 8km (5 miles).
Ascent: 980m (3215 feet).

From the end of the road go ahead for a short distance to a burn, heading upstream on its true right bank to a wall. Now keep to the left side of the wall to another burn, there following a narrow path on its left bank to ascend the moor ahead. As the burn finally expires, climb to the boulder-studded slopes that rise to the rim of Coire Fearchair, and from there make best use of the numerous large boulders to ease your progress. Because the slope is convex, the summit seems a long time coming, but as the boulders thin to grass, you know you are near.

From the edge of the summit plateau dominated by that imposing cairn, there is a stunning view of Broadford Bay and the near islands of Raasay, Scalpay and Pabay, beyond which the peaks of

Applecross and Torridon loom darkly on the horizon. Turning round you gain an extensive view across Skye with Bla Bheinn and the Red Cuillin holding front of stage.

The circuit continues to Beinn Dearg Mhór, reached from the south-western edge of the summit plateau, from where you descend easily to a neat bealach, now heading west. As you go so a more pronounced path materialises, rising to the stony summit of Beinn Dearg Mhór, from where the view of Bla Bheinn is outstanding and uninterrupted. The highest point is also marked by a substantial cairn.

The top of Beinn Dearg Mhór, however, is rather featureless, so the correct line for the start of the long scree descent to Bealach Coire Sgreamhach (south-east) requires good navigation. When descending this scree you will appreciate why, following my first clockwise circuit of this horseshoe, I decided to reverse this walk — 'purgatory' springs readily to mind.

Another large cairn awaits at the top of the ridge rising from the bealach to Beinn Dearg Bheag, along with a fine view down Loch Slapin to the Island of Rhum.

The final ridge flows eastwards from this final summit and is quite delightful, curving round Coire Gorm, and down which you can easily find a way through heather and boulders, aided some of the way by sheep tracks. As the ridge steepens, carefully descend heathery slopes, heading for the Allt Beinn Deirge, crossing it, and then following its true left bank, initially rough, but easing lower down as it bends to run north-eastwards. The onward route goes through an enclosure, beyond which you can return to the burn, and press on to Coire-chat-achan and your starting point.

WALK 2.3:
Beinn na Cro

This minor summit lies sandwiched between Srath Mór and Srath Beag at the head of Loch Slapin. Undeservedly, it is often neglected by walkers, lying as it does between higher neighbours, but provides a welcome period of solitude at the height of the season when other routes are busy. The ascent is simplest by its south ridge, a broad mix of grass, rock and scree, returning the same way.

Start/Finish: Head of Loch Slapin. GR.568220.
Distance: 4½km (3 miles).
Ascent: 570m (1879 feet).

Begin from the water's edge at Loch Slapin, not far from the new bridge spanning the Abhainn an t-Sratha Mhóir, choose a convenient line up the hill, and follow it. The gradient is not unduly demanding, but this modest ascent should not be treated casually. The summit gives good views of Belig to the west and Beinn na Caillich (east), and northwards to Loch Ainort, Loch na Cairidh and the island of Scalpay. Return by the same route.

For an alternative, and longer descent, continue north along the summit ridge until the gradient significantly eases, and then strike east, descending rough ground to the wide grassy bealach above An Slugan. From here you can turn southwards on a good path that runs down Srath Beag to Loch Slapin, reaching the road at Torrin, about 1km (½ mile) east of your starting point.

WALK 2.4:
Srath Mór and Srath Beag

The two glens of Srath Mór and Srath Beag both run north-south, yet link the east and west coast of the islands, such is the convoluted character of the Skye landscape. Between them they enclose a minor summit, Beinn na Cro (Walk 2.3), and provide a healthy bout of low-level walking that is not without appeal. Although the walk can be undertaken from four different starting points, it is vital to begin as recommended here, from near the bridge at the head of Loch Slapin. The reason is simple: the attractions of low-lying Srath Mór conceal an inordinate bogginess following rain, which may not have amused Prince Charlie when he chose this route across Skye in 1746, bound for the safety of France. Moreover, in times of spate it is impossible or dangerous to cross the Abhainn an t-Sratha Mhóir when the path switches sides. Given these possible obstacles to further progress, it is better to encounter them sooner rather than later, in order to effect the minimum retreat.

Start/Finish: Head of Loch Slapin, near Abhainn an t-Sratha Mhóir. GR.565224.
Distance: 17km (10½ miles).
Ascent: 260m (855 feet).

So, set off along the track into Srath Mór, soon passing Clach Oscar (Oscar's Stone), a large boulder tossed here by one of the legendary Fiennes in a moment of merriment. The track soon deteriorates to a path along the shores of Loch na Sguabaidh, and, after rain, is invariably found to be part of the loch.

Beyond the loch the path is in poor condition, and evading the worst clutches of the bogs will become a major pre-occupation. If all is dry, or frozen, the subsequent crossing of the glen river should not prove difficult.

The path never climbs higher than 17m (55 feet) above sea level, before dropping imperceptibly as it heads for Luib. Approaching this village, the path forks. Go right, taking the most direct route to the village, and on reaching the road, go immediately right, across the old bridge that once carried the Broadford-Portree road. It now climbs on to the slopes of Am Meall, north of Loch nam Madadh Uisge, and provides vastly better going, accompanied by fine coastal views, as far as the Allt Strollamus.

Leave the old road here, but do not cross the river, keeping instead to its east bank, along a path that climbs into the narrows of An Slugan. Rather more ascent is ahead of you now, rising to about 190m (623 feet) to reach a wide, grassy bealach where the path switches sides as in the neighbouring glen.

Now press on down Srath Beag, high above the true left bank of Allt an t-Sratha Bhig, to reach the road at Torrin, a short walk west to your starting point.

You can abridge the finish as you come out of Srath Beag by recrossing the Allt an t-Sratha Bhig high up, and cutting across rough ground directly to your starting point. This will avoid the road walk.

Loch na Sguabaidh

Loch na Sguabaidh was for years inhabited by a waterhorse whose principal occupation seems to have been carrying off any pretty girl who wandered within his reach. Plain lassies were thought to be safe enough; indeed, to have been captured by the waterhorse and to have escaped was to assure your reputation as a beauty. The waterhorse's taste for mischief, however, eventually led to his demise, as, en route to Loch na Creitheach, the beast was killed by MacKinnon of Strath in Bealach na Beiste (the Pass of the Beast).

WALK 2.5:
Suisnish and Boreraig

Few places on Skye bear such evident testimony to the ruthlessness that underpinned the Highland Clearances as the deserted villages of Suisnish and Boreraig. And though you could argue, as does Hamish MacInnes in West Highland Walks *(Two: Skye to Cape Wrath), that the Clearances were economically inevitable, there are many who hold scant regard for the manner in which it was done.*

This walk, which begins from the ruined church of Strath, at Kilchrist, visits both communities. It is a sad and poignant excursion, made palatable by outstanding coastal scenery.

Start/Finish: Kilchrist (Cill Chriosd) Church, Strath Suardal. GR.617207.
Distance: 16km (10 miles).
Ascent: 290m (950 feet).

To begin you need to walk along the narrow road, heading for Torrin and Kilbride, for about 2½km (1½ miles); a necessary evil, on which you need to take care against speeding traffic. As the road bends right, towards Kilbride, leave it by another back road on the left, that descends to the shores of Loch Slapin, there running south to the tiny cove of Camas Malag. A fine walk ensues, along a clear and broad track, built when the Board of Agriculture briefly re-crofted Suisnish during this century.

The track turns inland a little to negotiate Glen Boreraig, before resuming its southerly course for Suisnish. Once more the track turns inland as it crosses the Allt Poll a'Bhainne, near which the hut circle marked on the map is revealed as a pile of rocks on a slight rise. Further inland, the remains of Dun Kearstack stand atop a larger prominence. On closer inspection, you will find an entire village strung out along a rib of land, quite unsuspected from below.

Shortly after crossing the Allt Poll a'Bhainne, the track approaches Suisnish, with many field enclosures, and many of the former field boundaries still in evidence, a wide spread of good grassland, scarcely reclaimed by weeds. One ruined croft is rather more substantial than the others, and could provide emergency shelter. Beyond this the track runs on to a sheep washing station, where it effectively ends.

Past this station, a path, not easy to locate, heads for the top of a small sea cliff, before passing south of Carn Dearg, and descending to the shore and a natural rock pavement.

The on-going route is then never in doubt, and leads unerringly to Boreraig, passing two fine waterfalls en route, trekking below the southernmost, eagle-patrolled escarpments of Beinn Bhuidhe, described by David Craig as "blackish, degenerate stuff, a coagulation neither earth nor rock…crawling with ivy in their nether reaches. They piss soil and shit stones down spouting cascades of a horrible beauty, curving out of the ground at eighty or a hundred feet in twists of snow-white water, demon-haired".

As you enter the ruins of Boreraig, head for the conspicuous standing stone, almost central to the triangle of arable land that presses northwards into the flanks of Beinn a'Mheadhain, "smiling like an oasis".

Having explored the village return to the standing stone, and from it follow a fairly obvious path, north-east and north, passing more ruined dwellings, eventually to join a good, if wet, path above the Allt na Pairte. This path now strikes across the moors, and is rarely dry, and wettest in the vicinity of Loch Lonachan. But once past this dank spot, the going improves as it descends into Strath Suardal.

A number of paths lead down to the strath road, the most interesting taking you by way of a marble quarry, before emerging through willow scrub on to the road, not far from your starting point.

The Clearance of Suisnish and Boreraig

Ballingall, Lord MacDonald's factor, was the chief culprit, and in 1852 he and his henchmen, described as 'ground officers', found their way to these long-established communities where Loch Slapin and Loch Eishort meet.

If the crofters, mostly surnamed Macrae or MacInnes, offered resistance, they were forcibly evicted and their properties razed to the ground to prevent them from returning. One man, who did return to Suisnish, was found dead at the door of his ruined house the next morning, having perished from the cold during the night.

The people of Suisnish grew barley and potatoes, and had a few fishing boats. They used the braes of Beinn Bhuidhe as common grazing, and led a difficult and hard life.

Yet Lord MacDonald's factor argued that "he had been over-indulgent to this community, that he had allowed the people to waste good land, and that it would be better for them and it if they were removed". One of the evicting officers announced that in directing the evictions Lord MacDonald was "prompted by motives of benevolence, piety and humanity, because they were too far from the church".

Most of the people were sent to Campbeltown, where they were put aboard the Hercules by the Emigration Commissioners. Many died from smallpox, and on hearing this the thirty-two families left at Suisnish and Boreraig asked that they should be left to stay on Skye. They were threatened with eviction in the autumn of 1853.

A report in the Northern Ensign *said it all*: "The women and the children went about tearing their hair, and rending the heaven with their cries. Mothers with tender infants at the breast looked helplessly on, while their effects and their aged and infirm relatives were cast out, and the doors of their houses locked in their faces. No mercy was shown to age or sex, all were indiscriminately thrust out and left to perish". When the officers had gone, the women and children crept into the cattle byres and sheep pens, and waited. When their menfolk returned, some having been taken prisoner to Portree and then walked to Inverness to face trial, they opened the houses, restored the roofs, and rekindled the peat fires. But the joy was short-lived, for, five days after Christmas, Lord MacDonald's men returned again and turned out everyone, "and the snow fell on the little heaps of clothing, on the women and the children huddled against the walls".

Eighteen people were somehow still surviving at Boreraig and Suisnish when the spring of 1854 arrived, but by the first days of summer, the township was deserted. One of the last to leave was an old man of eighty-six. He said: "I have paid sixty-six rents to the MacDonalds, and I am not one farthing in arrears. To be cast out of my house and my home to make room for...sheep is what I never expected. It is breaking my heart".

But from the few accounts of these evictions that can be found, none but one mentions the despicable thing the ground officers did with the milk. In his valuable and deeply-researched book On the Crofters' Trail, writer David Craig recounts the experience of a boy who lived at Boreraig, as explained by his daughter.

"He remembered the bailiffs putting out the fire with the basins of milk — you know that they set the milk for cream to make butter, and I suppose a small boy would remember that, because in those days milk was very precious".

Not by any stretch of imagination could such an act be described as the Lord showing "benevolence, piety and humanity".

Heading for Bla Bheinn along the north bank of the Allt na Dunaiche

WALK 2.6:
Bla Bheinn

O Blaaven, rocky Blaaven
How I long to be with you again,
To see lashed gulf and gully
Smoke white in the windy rain —
To see in the scarlet sunrise
The mist-wreaths perish with heat,
The wet rock slide with a trickling gleam
Right down to the cataract's feet.

(*Blaaven*, Alexander Smith)

Once the magnificence of Bla Bheinn has been experienced first hand, few who make the ascent would argue with Alexander Nicolson's view that it is the finest hill on Skye. Others are higher, or have more demanding ascents, but Bla Bheinn is a law unto itself. Nicolson was a Skye man who explored the Island extensively, and but one among many to eulogise upon the virtues of the mountain.

Those who perceive Bla Bheinn as merely an appendage to the main Cuillin range will be surprised by a journey down the Elgol road, along which, once Loch Cill Chriosd is reached, the mountain's eastern aspect is viewed with ever-growing and independent grandeur, beautiful at all times, quite wonderful beneath a mantle of snow when the nival buttresses rise grandly into cloud.

Bla Bheinn is the highest and most southerly of the Cuillin Outliers, and links with the westernmost Red Cuillin in a continuous chain of hills from the southern tip of Strathaird to Sligachan. Such a link, for non-scramblers, is however thwarted by the impossibility of Clach Glas, though the ascent of Bla Bheinn, and many of the other summits, independently, offers more than ample compensation.

The eastern side of Bla Bheinn is accessible from the Broadford-Elgol road, while the south ridge can be reached from Camasunary and/or Kilmarie. The mountain has two summits, about 300 m/yds apart, the lower (by a couple of metres) lying at the culminating point of the south ridge. Between the two lies a narrow linking col, at the head of the Great Scree Gully (south-east) and Willink's Gully (west-

north-west). Opinions vary, according to the scrambling/rock climbing ability of the writer, as to the ease with which the traverse from the south summit to the main top (or vice versa) may be accomplished. The difficulties lie on the south summit side of the col. The Scottish Mountaineering Club Guide (The Islands of Scotland including Skye) *describes this obstacle as "a 15m step down", another book describes this as "a simple if slightly exposed scramble along a ledge". Although the crossing is rather easier north to south, it remains intimidating. If you suffer from any degree of exposure, it is out of bounds; likewise, if you have no scrambling experience. Walkers ascending by the south ridge (the easiest ascent) may have to consider satisfying themselves with the marginally lower summit, from which the view, especially of the main Cuillin ridge, is no less spectacular. Munro-baggers who have not yet faced the intricacies of the Inaccessible Pinnacle on Sgurr Dearg, and all other walkers bound for the highest point, will find the ascent from the east the best way of adding the summit to their list.*

2.6a: East Ridge

Start/Finish: Small parking area (GR.561218), near bridge over Allt na Dunaiche, 1km (½ mile) beyond the head of Loch Slapin.
Distance: 8km (5 miles).
Ascent: 915m (3000 feet).

From the roadside, follow the good path that runs along the north bank of the Allt na Dunaiche, weaving through a wooded gorge and around heathery hummocks, and passing some fine waterfalls en route. The great grey cliffs of Bla Bheinn are always ahead, flanked, on the right, by those of Clach Glas and Sgurr nan Each.

Further on, cross the Allt na Dunaiche, beyond which the path starts trending to the left to reach a tributary stream at the foot of Coire Uaigneich. A mix of grass and loose stone lies ahead, now ascending more strenuously as you continue past a large buttress that forms the end of the east ridge. Soon you reach the upper part of the corrie, with Loch Fionna-choire and the satellite, An Stac, off to the east, and the Great Scree Gully directly above you. For much of the way the path is clear and cairned, though once the upper

Approaching the summit of Bla Bheinn by the East Ridge

corrie is reached, both become less obvious. The cairns that do appear lead to the Great Scree Gully, and, in poor visibility, this in spite of its rubbishy condition is the surest line of ascent and descent.

Now swing round to the right and tackle steep grass and rocks to gain the east ridge. There are a number of possible lines, all reaching the broad crest of the ridge at some point; once this is achieved, the onward route is much more evident, and ascends through stony grooves and up rocky buttresses to a spectacular view of Clach Glas between the walls of an intervening gully.

Continue ascending, with more views of Clach Glas to attract the camera, before progressing upwards on a clearly-trodden path with a little (avoidable) easy scrambling en route, before finally emerging on the summit shoulder, with only a short, easy walk up to the trig point and cairn remaining. The view of the Cuillin that greets the last few strides, assuming you have been blessed with clear weather, is breathtaking and sudden, and matched only by that of the great gullies sweeping down from your feet into Glen Sligachan.

To return, you must retrace your steps, though this may prove difficult and potentially dangerous in misty conditions. If mists do suddenly appear, head for the col between the two summits and descend the Great Scree Gully, with care.

An alternative awaits those who can cross to the south summit, then descending the long and splendid south ridge until you can branch left across the Abhainn nan Leac to reach the track linking Camasunary and Kilmarie, following this out to the Broadford road, and a return roadwalk of some 6+km (4 miles).

2.6b: South Ridge

Start/Finish: Roadside parking, Kilmarie. GR.545172.
Distance: 13km (8 miles).
Ascent: 1008m (3305 feet).

Opposite the parking space at Kilmarie a gate/stile gives on to a broad track heading across a rugged landscape and crossing a number of streams at fords. The view, right, over Abhainn Cille Mhaire is of Slat Bheinn, which initially obscures that of Bla Bheinn. Directly ahead, across the col of Am Màm and Sgurr na Stri beyond, rise the dark summits of the Black Cuillin.

Am Màm is marked by a large cairn, and a short way further on, as the track bends, so the enormous south ridge of Bla Bheinn looms into view.

Descend the on-going track, now with the bay of Camasunary below, and the rugged beauty of Glen Sligachan ahead. Before reaching a hairpin bend, leave the track at a small cairn, for a narrow path that cuts across to the Abhainn nan Leac. Soon after crossing this stream, leave the path and head up the hillside to gain the crest of the south ridge from the east.

Once on the ridge, what remains, albeit considerable, is immensely satisfying, a fine upward romp, swinging this way and that to avoid countless minor bumps and in-pressing gullies, though only modest scrambling ability is needed to tackle all the gabbro outcrops head on. The lower part of the ridge is grassy and leads to more cragginess higher up. The path bypasses all the difficulties, and finally places you at the large cairn on the south summit. The onward crossing to the main top negotiates the awkward col described earlier.

Allt na Dunaiche
The Allt na Dunaiche is variously called the 'Burn of Sorrow', or the 'Burn of Misfortune', an appellation that alludes to a tale of seven girls and a young boy who went to spend the summer in a shieling up above the waterfall, where the burn rises. One day, the girls went out to a wedding, leaving the boy alone. During his lonely vigil, the shieling was entered by seven large cats, who seated themselves by the fire, and talked. They boy watched, spellbound. Then the cats arose, took all the goodness from the butter and the cream, leaving but the appearance of goodness, and vanished. When the girls came home, and the terrified child recounted the story, the girls, seeing what appeared to be butter and cream in plenty, laughed at him, saying it was a dream. Next night, back came the cats, and by dawn light all the girls were dead. Later that day, when their mothers came to fetch the butter and cream, as was customary, each, as they entered the shieling and saw the dead girls, cried out "Airidh mo dunach" (the Shieling of Misfortune).

WALK 2.7:
Sgurr nan Each

Were it not for an infuriating rock pinnacle along its west ridge, it would be possible for walkers to combine Sgurr nan Each with the adjacent summits of Garbh-bheinn and Belig. As it is, the non-climber must be content with but a single summit as reward for effort. That route too is preordained, and must go by the south-east ridge.

Start/Finish: Bridge over Allt na Dunaiche, 1km (½ mile) beyond the head of Loch Slapin; parking a short distance further on at GR.561218.
Distance: 5km (3 miles).
Ascent: 725m (2380 feet).

Set off along the path on the north bank of the Allt na Dunaiche, as described in Walk 2.6, and after the waterfalls are reached (or sooner if you feel so inclined), head across the rough intervening ground, northwards, to gain the foot of the south-east ridge.

The ascent starts easily enough on grass and heather, but steepens, and becomes rocky as the east top is approached. A short dip from the east top, above a broad scree run on the north side of the mountain, leads to more rockwork on firm gabbro, climbing gradually to the summit.

On the return journey, do not be tempted by the grassy slope running south from the dip between the two tops; this only leads into difficulty far greater than retracing your steps.

WALK 2.8:
Garbh-bheinn

Lying only a short distance north of Bla Bheinn, the shapely summit of Garbh-bheinn receives rather less attention than its more spectacular neighbours. Its northern ridge proper is preceded by another long ridge rising from the head of Loch Ainort, the Druim Eadar Dà Choire, which also provides the finest way down. The walk is quite simply outstanding in good conditions, and shows off the main Cuillin, the Cuillin Outliers and the Red Hills to splendid effect.

Start/Finish: Lay-by near bend on A850, at head of Loch Ainort. GR.537265.
Distance: 8km (5 miles).
Ascent: 845m (2770 feet).

From the road bend set off across the heathery moorland finger poked between the Allt Coire nam Bruadaran and the Abhainn Ceann Loch Ainort, the former producing, close by the road, the white gash of a fine waterfall, Eas a'Bhradain, largely fed by the waters that flow from the gathering grounds of Coire nam Bruadaran, below Marsco.

The moorland rises easily to the long, boulder-strewn ridge of Druim Eadar Dà Choire, the eastern flank of Coire nam Bruadaran, but if you remain close to the Abhainn Ceann Loch Ainort for a while you can inspect a number of small waterfalls. Once beyond these move upwards and half right to gain the ridge, then climbing to the grassy top at 489m (1604 feet), from where there is a spectacular view of the main Cuillin ridge.

From this intermediate top, set off south-east, following a line of rusting fence posts, and descending about 60m (200 feet) to a col where a change in the colour of the rock clearly marks the boundary between the Red and Black Cuillin. Beyond, still following fence posts, ascend the crest of the north ridge proper, a satisfying and straight-forward experience. Higher up grass dominates the ridge for a while, before steepening once more. A left turn, now heading east, brings some easy rock work along a shattered and very narrow ridge to reach the main summit, marked by a cairn.

Return by the same route, with the bulk of Marsco swelling beyond Am Fraoch-choire. If you want to explore Coire nam Bruadaran, go left (west) from the top of Druim Eadar Dà Choire (489m: 1604 feet) and descend to the bealach at 323m (1060 feet), from there heading north into Coire nam Bruadaran, for an arduous and invariably wet tussle to regain the A850.

From the top of Garbh-bheinn it is possible to descend the north-east ridge to reach the Bealach na Beiste, where one of the MacKinnons killed the legendary beast that inhabited Loch na Sguabaidh (see Walk 2.4). The ridge descends abruptly from the summit of the mountain, being rocky to start, but soon progressing to a steep and bouldery slope before broadening out into a boulder-strewn shoulder just above the bealach. You need to take care on this descent, which is awkward in a few places, being a

Garbh-bheinn

combination of angled rock and loose gravelly scree. As you approach the bealach, a few gullies intrude, but these can be avoided by keeping to the crown of the ridge.

From the bealach you can either go north, again through disagreeable terrain, or, the only sensible reason for coming this way, ascend Belig. The lower slopes of Belig are rather scree-ridden, but the worst of this can be evaded by resorting to an easier line up adjacent rocky ribs. When you encounter a dilapidated dyke, follow this up the narrowing ridge to the neat summit.

WALK 2.9:
Belig

Although Belig can be ascended from Loch Ainort, usually combined with Glas Bheinn Mhór, an approach from the south, starting from the head of Loch Slapin is both shorter and more beautiful, in particular providing an opportunity to explore the Allt Aigeann. This approach also facilitates a short circular tour, ascending by the south-east ridge and descending by the south-west.

The western slopes of the mountain are gabbro, with good frictional qualities; the upper reaches, however, turn to basalt, which is rather less adhesive, and quite slippery when wet.

Start/Finish: Head of Loch Slapin, west of the new bridge. GR.564225.
Distance: 7km (4½ miles).
Ascent: 700m (2295 feet).

From the bridge set off northwards until you reach the point where the Allt Aigeann flows underground (except after prolonged wet weather). If you can, cross the stream at this point, though if it is in spate you will have to detour west along its banks until you can safely cross. Progress on either bank is along sheep tracks. Just above the point where the stream bends, the transition from lower to upper glen is marked by a tiered waterfall, and a string of pools and mini-cascades that will waylay photographers, possibly all day.

The grassy going underfoot continues on to the south-east ridge, climbing steeply to a gathering of small outcrops, through which more sheep tracks thread a route. Higher up, the terrain is rockier and leads to a rock tower, that scramblers can tackle head on, while walkers will find an easier option on the right. Above this tower, the ridge narrows appreciably to provide simple rockwork with the occasional sense of exposure. All the difficulties, such as they are, can be avoided.

Just before the final rise to the summit you cross a short grassy stretch, a good spot for a halt, with fine views to far Trotternish.

Keep on across the summit, and descend the south-west ridge to Bealach na Beiste, a broad col that separates Belig from Garbh-bheinn. The way across the summit and down the ridge follows a dilapidated dyke, and an intermittent path just off the crest on the right. The lower section is broad, bouldery and awkward.

From the bealach, turn south-east and descend broken slopes (with care) into the corrie that feeds the Allt Aigeann. As you descend, keeping to the true left bank of the stream, so the going improves, and the charm of this remote corrie slowly unfolds. The many pools and cascades mentioned earlier must rank this stretch of the walk among the most beautiful on Skye, and worth the ascent of Belig on that account alone.

WALK 2.10:
Glas Bheinn Mhór

Not unlike its neighbour, Beinn na Cro across Srath Mór, the elongated ridge of Glas Bheinn Mhór has all the appearance of a dull and uninteresting heap of scree and boulders. Were it not for the view it offers, especially of Loch Ainort, Raasay and beyond, it would be far more neglected than it is. On a fine summer's day, however,

Opposite: Sgurr nan Gillian from Allt Dearg Mhor

The southern Cuillin from Bruach na Frithe

Sgurr na h-Uamha from the main Cuillin Ridge

*walkers in search of solitude will find it here, in return for little more
than a steady plod.*

Start/Finish: A850, east of Luib. GR.560279.
Distance: 5km (3 miles).
Ascent: 540m (1770 feet).

From the roadside, locate a ruined wall climbing up the northern
ridge of Glas Bheinn Mhór, and head for it. Once you have reached
the wall, ascend pleasantly in its company to the summit.
Return the same way.

WALK 2.11:
South Ainort Circular

*The three preceding walks explain how to tackle individually the
summits of Garbh-bheinn, Belig and Glas Bheinn Mhór, but strong
walkers, on a fine day, would have no difficulty combining all three in
an outstanding circular tour from Loch Ainort. Unless extra transport
is arranged, the walk will start or finish with a stretch of road walking
along Loch Ainort, but an interest in the wildfowl that frequent these
coastal waters will enliven the journey.*

Start/Finish: A850, east of Luib. GR.560279.
Distance: 13km (8 miles), with 3km (2 miles) road walking.
Ascent: 1285m (4215 feet).

Begin with the ascent of Glas Bheinn Mhór from Luib, as described
in Walk 2.10, and from the summit continue in a south-westerly
direction, following a dilapidated dyke across the connecting col with
Belig, before climbing a scree and boulder slope to reach Belig a
little to the east of the main summit.
Following the summital dyke over Belig and down to the Bealach
na Beiste, from there ascending the lower, broad bouldery slopes of
Garbh-bheinn, rising to awkward slabs and gravel near the finely-
honed summit.

Keep going west for a short distance to reach the top of the north ridge of Garbh-bheinn, and there descend northwards, keeping as much as possible to the highest ground to avoid scree, and following a line of rusting fence posts. The col below the neatly-shaped top of the Druim Eadar Dà Choire marks a clear geological boundary between Red and Black Cuillin.

Climb to the top of the ridge, still following fence posts, and, with Loch Ainort and the Red Cuillin before you, and the Black Cuillin stacked on the port side, set off down the ridge and across the lower moorland to reach the A850. A simple walk along the road will bring you easily back to Luib.

WALK 2.12:
Marsco

This distinctive summit is one of the finest sights among the high mountains of Skye; its very isolation gives its bold, sweeping lines great appeal, especially when viewed across the peat-stained waters of the River Sligachan.

Marsco is usually climbed from Sligachan, from where you can combine two routes to form a circular walk, arduous and unrelenting, but eminently satisfying. An alternative approach ascends through Coire nam Bruadaran from the shores of Loch Ainort, remote and pathless for most of the way, where the feeling of isolation grows with every forward step, and the spirits of the past creep up on you.

There are no difficulties to either ascent, but expect energetic walking from start to finish. Unlike neighbouring summits, very little scree is encountered on Marsco.

2.12a From Sligachan

Start/Finish: Sligachan. GR.487299.
Distance: 12½km (8 miles).
Ascent: 745m (2445 feet).

This approach tackles the north ridge first and returns through the

Coire Dubh Measarroch, but may be just as easily reversed.

From the old bridge at Sligachan, take the track between the River Sligachan and the Allt Daraich that runs into Glen Sligachan for 3km (2 miles) until you reach the Allt na Measarroch, just before which there are the remains of an old deer fence. Cross the burn, and turn left (east) along its true left bank. [NOTE: If you are reversing these directions, do not cross the burn, but stay on an indistinct path into Coire Dubh Measarroch (the route almost certainly taken by Prince Charlie on his journey across Skye) between the burn and the deer fence remains.]

Follow the Allt na Measarroch eastwards for a short distance, until you feel you can branch away to tackle the northern slopes of Marsco. Then simply head up the ridge, first to the slight northern top, and then, across a slight dip and an easier gradient, to the main summit, marked by a small cairn, and its magnificent panorama. You can expect hard work at all times once you reach the ridge, and a number of false summits.

Harta Corrie and the main Cuillin ridge understandably dominate the summit view to the west, while southwards you take in Ruadh Stac, Garbh-bheinn and Bla Bheinn and the view down Glen Sligachan to Sgurr na Stri. Over on Raasay, Dun Caan is well seen from Marsco.

Continue across the summit, heading south-east, and descending just over 100m (300 feet) to a small col just before the minor south-east summit. Here you will meet the old deer fence encountered earlier, which has found a way through Coire Dubh Measarroch and Coire nan Laogh to gain the ridge.

Now turn north, descending with the fence on your left, down through Coire nan Laogh, crossing the deep ravine of the burn that flows from the corrie en route, to the broad bealach, Màm a'Phobuill, where you can cross the infant Allt na Measarroch, thereafter heading down the Coire between burn and fence remains back to Glen Sligachan.

2.12b From Loch Ainort

Start/Finish: Eas a'Bhradain, A850. GR.534266.
Distance: 8½km (5¼ miles).
Ascent: 715m (2345 feet).

Follow the path on the true left bank of the Allt Coire nam Bruadaran, and climb above Eas a'Bhradain, a spectacular fall, especially when the burn is in spate. Sadly, this foaming exclamation mark beneath the Corrie of Dreams must instantly suffer the ignominy of a concrete culvert as it is forced beneath the road that other, less sensitive, needs demanded.

The path through heather into the corrie is not distinct, barely more than a sheep trod, but climbs beside the vivid burn, before rising to the bealach (Point 323) between Marsco and the neat top of the Druim Eadar Dà Choire.

During the ascent, the great shawl of Marsco inhibits views of the Cuillin world beyond, its shoulder decorated by the perfectly-formed jewel of Coire nam Laogh, the Corrie of the Calves. As you head into the corrie, you need to cross the Allt Màm a'Phobuill, then ascend rough ground to the bealach at the foot of Marsco's south-east ridge. Here you encounter the rusted remains of a deer fence, which can be followed in a north-westerly direction on to the south-east ridge, ascending steeply, but without difficulty. Higher up, relief comes in the form of a narrow grassy ridge as the fenceposts drop north-wards into Coire nan Laogh.

All that remains, after a short dip, is a steady plod up an easy slope to the narrow summit.

Return to the dip where the old deer fence drops into Coire nan Laogh, and follow the fence down, northwards, to the broad bealach, Màm a'Phobuill, where you leave the fence to cross the Allt Màm a'Phobuill, as high as possible (ideally at the bealach), then following its true left (north) bank eastwards into Coire nam Bruadaran where you will rejoin your outward route.

Coire nam Bruadaran

The 'Corrie of Dreams' has origins lost in time; no one knows what dream was brought to bear on this shallow, shadowy wilderness. It is the first real gateway into the Cuillin, but one hastily overlooked by the frenetics bound for Sligachan and the spoils of the Black Cuillin. With nothing now to advise of its creation, you could do far worse than accept for Coire nam Bruadaran the tale cleverly related in Jim Crumley's evocative book, The Heart of Skye.

Màm a'Phobuill

Although shown on maps as Màm a'Phobuill, the Pass of the People, there is a local tradition that this broad bealach is known as The Prince's Pass, Màm a'Phrionnsa, adding weight to the contested theory that the Prince's route did indeed lie through the glen between Marsco and Beinn Dearg Mheadhonach and into Coire nam Bruadaran, the Corrie of Dreams.

WALK 2.13:
The Beinn Deargs

Viewed from Sligachan, the two Beinn Deargs, Mhor and Mheadhonach, lie between the formidable scree pile of Glamaig and the shapely form of Marsco. Tackled anticlockwise they offer one of the easiest (a relative term) walks in the Red Cuillin, and can, by energetic souls, be combined with Glamaig to provide a long day out. The key to the ascent is the long, curving ridge, Druim na Ruaige, that folds a protective arm around Am Fuar-choire.

Start/Finish: Sligachan. GR.487299.
Distance: 10½km (6½ miles).
Ascent: 875m (2870 feet).

Take the Coruisk Path from Sligachan for a short distance, as far as a split boulder at a diverging path along the Allt Daraich, confined here to a deep gorge that leads to an attractive waterfall. Before reaching the waterfall, head away from the burn, go round a small brae, and then head across open moorland targeting the prominent lump of Sron a'Bhealain, at the northern end of Druim na Ruaige.

The climb to Sron a'Bhealain is grassy and steep, and culminates in a fine viewpoint. This ascent alone is an excellent snippet to squeeze in at the end of a rainy day when frustration levels are high, and as often happens the skies clear for an hour or two.

Beyond Sron a'Bhealain, the grassy walking along Druim na

Ruaige, high above Glen Sligachan, is excellent, finally becoming a steep, cairned path through scree that rises to the top of Beinn Dearg Mheadhonach, the highest point of which lies a short distance south-east along the shattered and narrow summital ridge, which has a cairn at each end.

Go back along the ridge to begin a superb descent to Bealach Mosgaraidh beyond which Beinn Dearg Mhor leans against the backdrop of Glamaig. Viewed end on the scree slope rising from the bealach appears daunting, but succumbs rather more easily than expected, by a path zigzagging hesitantly up scree slopes. As a vantage point, the summit is as good as any among the Red Cuillin, and provides a breathtaking view eastwards over Loch Ainort to Scalpay, and northwards to Raasay.

From the summit, descend northwards for about ½km (550 yards) until, just before the final, minor top you can turn down the steep bouldery slope to Bealach na Sgairde. The descent is loose in many places but, equally, is liberally endowed with large, stable boulders, that make progress a little less tiring.

To return to Sligachan from Bealach na Sgairde, you must now

The Red Cuillin viewed from the summit of Bla Bheinn

descend more scree, though far less demanding, into the upper reaches of Coire na Sgairde. As you reach the lower glen, follow the Allt Bealach na Sgairde to its confluence with the Allt Daraich, near a deer fence. It is usually better to cross both burns at this point, then follow a narrow path on the true left bank of the Allt Daraich back to its waterfalls and attractively wooded gorge, and the old bridge at Sligachan.

WALK 2.14:
Glamaig

Rising boldly from the shores of Loch Sligachan, Glamaig works hard to win attention for itself and the other smooth-profiled Red Hills, but suffers badly by having nothing but interminable scree in its shop window, and that faces Sligachan, vying for your attention with the dark, pinnacled spires of Sgurr nan Gillean and company. It is the highest and most northerly of the Red Cuillin and forms an elongated grassy ridge with a summit at each end. Overlooking Sligachan, Sgurr Mhairi is the summit of the mountain, while north-east lies An Coileach.

Exceptional quantities of enthusiasm, none of which will have any foundation in reason, will be needed if you are to tackle the Glamaig diretissima from Sligachan. A less demanding option lies in approaching Glamaig along its north-east ridge, passing first over An Coileach before tramping the ridge to the summit. This is the only ascent that avoids scree, though some will be encountered on the return, which here is suggested by way of the Bealach na Sgairde.

Start/Finish: A850, 400m/yds south of the Moll road. GR.536315.
Distance: 6½km (4 miles).
Ascent: 795m (2610 feet).

Begin at the end of the fence by the road, where it turns through a right-angle to head uphill. The fence deteriorates to fence posts as you climb. Stay with the fenceline until above a rock outcrop, when

71

you can more conveniently gain the main ridge line. Any scree encountered en route can largely be avoided on rock or grass, which rises steeply to a defensive group of outcrops just below An Coileach.

Beyond this eastern summit, the ridge, still adorned with fence posts, begins with a short dip before climbing again to the higher top. When the fence posts change direction, leave them, and head directly for the summit trig. The cairn of Sgurr Mhairi lies a short way further on, and provides one of Skye's most outstanding viewpoints.

Although Sgurr nan Gillean and its brethren dominate the view to the south-west, Glamaig still provides a vast panorama, from the Outer Isles to Ben Nevis. Closer at hand lie Loch Bracadale, the long swelling of the Trotternish ridge, the whole of Raasay, and, to the south, Bla Bheinn, more than justifying its claim to be by far the most attractive mountain on Skye.

You can retreat by your outward route, but by way of extending the journey a little, you might descend first to Bealach na Sgairde. Do not, however, make a bee-line for it directly from the Sgurr Mhairi cairn; the ridge is confusing at this point. Backtrack as far as the trig, and then move half right to intercept that line of old fence posts, following them until they make a sharp turn. From this corner, descend south-south-east to reach the scree run above the bealach, the grassy haven of which soon comes into view.

Once the bealach is reached go down easy slopes to the east, making use of sheep tracks, and keeping well to the north of the burn, and (lower down) on grass above the heather. Only the last 15 minutes or so cause any difficulty, as your route crosses rough, hummocky and awkward terrain, following the line of the electricity pylons that despoil this broad, ruggedly handsome glen: good views across to Raasay compensate.

Havildar Harkabir Thapa

If you find the assault on Glamaig wearisome, reflect on the achievements of Havildar Harkabir Thapa, a Gurkha, who in 1899 ran from the door of the Sligachan Hotel to the summit of Glamaig, and back, in an astounding 55 minutes (37 up and 18 down). Although reliably attested, many doubted the possibility of this achievement, the more so because it was done barefoot. Since then, 56 years later, George Rhodes went up in 37½ minutes and down in 19, only marginally longer, wearing lightweight sports shoes of the day.

The Ghurka's record, however, no longer stands, though a Ghurka did win the race in 1995. The current record, held by Billy Rogers, is 46 minutes 2 seconds and was set in 1990; challengers must be fit, fast, inordinately strong, and possessed of that quaint element of eccentricity that hallmarks all good fell-runners.

If you don't measure up, forget it!

WALK 2.15:
Glen Sligachan

Anyone in search of a long low-level walk will find nothing better on Skye than the north-south gash of Glen Sligachan. Easing past the scree-decked hills of the Red Cuillin, then forcing a wet and weary way through the pressing walls of the Black Cuillin and their outliers, this monument of creation seems in certain light and weather conditions to be a direct and thinly-disguised highway to Hell.

Used principally as a means of reaching Loch Coruisk, the continuation runs on to the delightful bay at Camasunary, where escape lies to Kilmarie, across the high moorland bealach, Am Màm, or on to Elgol, reached by a superb promenade above the sea cliffs that form the western boundary of Beinn Leacach and Ben Cleat.

The route given here presupposes that the walker will either return to Sligachan (quite a day, doubling the distance given below), arrange transport to Kilmarie or Elgol (most appropriate), or try to coincide with the intermittent bus service between Broadford and Elgol (likely to put you under pressure if you slip behind schedule).

Progress through Glen Sligachan is invariably affected by the recent weather. After heavy or sustained rain, expect to ford many unaccommodating burns (or make tiring detours) and to plod along through what seems like an 8-mile long bog. In good conditions, expect much the same, but with midges.

The walking nevertheless ranks as magnificent in any conditions. If returning to Sligachan, you should plan to turn round when you have half had enough.

Start: Sligachan. GR.487299.
Finish: Camasunary. GR.515187 — with walking yet to do.
Distance: 12½km (7¾ miles).
Ascent: 100m (330 feet) — in many undulations.

Just beyond the old bridge at Sligachan, take the signposted path
for Loch Coruisk. The path, dominated in its early stages by the tower
of Sgurr nan Gillean, heads on relentlessly into the glen, encountering numerous feeder burns before reaching the rather more
substantial Allt na Measarroch. Cross the burn, almost always a wet
proposition, and continue to a prominent boulder, Clach na Craoibhe
Chaoruinn.

More pleasant walking beneath the great slopes of Marsco bring
you to a branching of ways, not far past the two Lochan Dubha, and
at the entrance to Am Fraoch-choire. To the west as you approach
the twin lochans you gain a glimpse through Harta Corrie to the dark
central peaks of the Black Cuillin.

The right fork heads for Druim Hain and Loch Coruisk or Sgurr
na Stri (see Walk 3.20), while the continuation of the glen route
runs on first to Loch an Athain and into the dramatic Srath na
Crèitheach. Beneath the long south ridge of Bla Bheinn, the path
passes close by Loch na Crèitheach before pressing on to reach
Camas Fhionnairigh (anglicised to Camasunary), one of the most
endearing places on the entire island, and an entirely relaxing
place to be. Here a wide sandy beach runs into a bright green sward
of meadow on which two buildings, one a bothy, the other private,
provide a stark contrast to the background darkness of Sgurr na Stri
and Bla Bheinn.

To the east, a broad track can be seen slanting up and across the
hillside to a low bealach, Am Màm, and this option, rough underfoot
but a broad track all the way, will take you out to the Elgol-Broadford
road at Kilmarie.

Less obvious is the fine clifftop path that runs south along the
coastline, across the Rubha na h'Airighe Bàine, the entrance to
Glen Scaladal, and along the cliffs below Ben Cleat to Elgol. This
extension is described in Walk 2.17, but makes a fine finish to a walk
through Glen Sligachan that strong walkers will enjoy.

WALK 2.16:
Kilmarie to Camasunary

For one of the most dramatic surprise views on the Island, you can do little better than follow the track from Kilmarie to Am Màm, the broad bealach due east of the bay of Camasunary. Whether you subsequently descend to Camasunary is largely irrelevant, though few I suspect could resist such a provocative temptation. What outstands is the noble rise of Bla Bheinn's south ridge, the dark pinnacles of the Black Cuillin across Srath na Crèitheach, the green sward below flush against its sandy beach and set against the rugged profile of Sgurr na Stri. Across Loch Scavaig, the island of Rhum sails darkly across the horizon, beyond the squat hour-glass shape of Soay. There are few places where the essence of Skye, the savage interplay of mountain and sea, wild glen and foreshore, the remoteness, is so well exemplified.

At the roadside at Kilmarie, a plaque announces

TRACK TO CAMASUNARY CONSTRUCTED
BY
M SQUADRON & 107 FIELD SQUADRON
75 ENGINEER REGIMENT (VOLUNTEERS)
JUNE 1968

Sadly, this endeavour was less altruistic than might be supposed, the plan being to 'improve' the route around the coastline from Camasunary to Loch Coruisk, to make access easier for anglers. The plan meant the destruction of the infamous Bad Step, a steep and unavoidable slab of rock directly above the sea. The climbing world objected most strongly, and the Bad Step survived, which is more than can be said for the bridge that formerly spanned the Abhainn Camas Fhionnairigh; what remained of it was taken down in the 1980s.

Start: Kilmarie, Kirkibost. GR.545172. Roadside parking.
Finish: Camasunary.
Distance: 4km (2½ miles) each way.
Ascent: Kilmarie to Am Màm: 150m (490 feet).
Camasunary to Am Màm: 190m (625 feet).

The route to Am Màm is never in doubt, a broad track that begins from the gate opposite the parking space. Just as you start, if you are blessed with a good day, you can pick out the higher of the Black Cuillin peaks beyond the bealach.

Crossing a couple of minor fords en route, the track, stony and uncomfortable underfoot in places, climbs to a cairn marking the top of the pass, and a short way further on starts to descend, heading into the view described earlier. The white buildings of Camasunary dot the vivid greenness of the coastal margin, and when caught by sunlight, contrast starkly with the dark gullies and crags of Sgurr na Stri.

Shortcuts on the way down do nothing other than nominally hasten your progress and add needlessly to a growing problem of erosion. Speed is not here of the essence; to consume at a leisurely pace the unadulterated splendour of the setting, is.

Walk 2.17 describes a continuation from Camasunary to Elgol, which combined with this walk, and about 5km (3 miles) of road walking (if a lift cannot be contrived), gives an excellent circuit.

WALK 2.17:
Camasunary to Elgol

Although often used in reverse as the first stage of the coastal path to Loch Coruisk, the section of clifftop walking between Elgol and Camasunary was relegated to a supporting role when cast against the briefer and less troublesome walk-in from Kilmarie that came into being in the late 1960s. Walkers with no intention of seeking out the confines of Coruisk, and who can accommodate airy, clifftop walking on a sometimes narrow and frequently wet path, will find the linking of Kilmarie, Camasunary and Elgol, in either direction, an exhilarating exercise.

Described here from north to south, this walk will serve as an appendage both to Walk 2.16 (Kilmarie to Camasunary) or Walk 2.15 (Glen Sligachan).

Start: Camasunary.
Finish: Elgol.
Distance: 6 km (3¾ miles).
Ascent: 180m (590 feet).

As you walk away from the buildings at Camasunary, a path materialises that leads you directly to a crossing of the Abhainn nan Leac at a ford, beyond which the on-going path runs across a boggy stretch of ground to start climbing above the sea cliffs. If the burn is in spate, you cannot cross at this point, and need to follow the track up to a bridge, from there returning along the course of the burn to locate the path. Any attempt to shortcut this little loop will get you very wet.

The path improves as it climbs above Rubha na h-Airighe Bàine, a low cliff that sports a good, if rather stunted assortment of trees – silver birch, goat willow, hazel, ash, holly and the occasional white poplar. With a couple of awkward steps down, the path eventually runs on to descend steeply through bracken to a spread of iris at Cladach a'Ghlinne, the entrance to Glen Scaladal. (NOTE: In an emergency Glen Scaladal can be used as an escape route back to Kilmarie – see below.)

Ford the burn issuing from Glen Scaladal, and locate the on-going path as it rises to tackle to cliffs below Ben Cleat. What follows is another helping of superb clifftop walking, from which you can gaze out across Loch Scavaig to Soay, Eigg, Rhum and Canna, with Camasunary and the Black Cuillin always there when you look back.

The path is continuous throughout, but wet and slippery in places. As it reaches the boundary fence of Elgol, climb steeply upwards beside the fence for a short distance to a gate, from which a track runs, right, to reach the road. If heading for Elgol's bouldery shore (or the toilets), turn right. If returning by road to Kilmarie, turn left.

Elgol

Linked to Broadford by a post bus service that runs twice daily, Elgol is very much the end of the road, lying almost at the tip of the Strathaird peninsula. Here you will find a post office and a few small shops, and accommodation. Best known for its dramatic, if distant, views of the Cuillin, the setting off point for boat trips to Loch Coruisk, and its point of access to the cave in which *Prince Charles Edward* spent his last night on Skye, Elgol is a timeless place in a timeless setting.

According to tradition, *Vortigern* despatched his lieutenant *Aella* and five ships to 'explore' (something of a carte blanche) the Western Isles. Resistant to 'exploration' the people of Skye raised what ships they could and intercepted *Aella* at the entrance to Loch Scavaig and engaged him in battle. *Aella*'s ships were driven off, but his name remains enshrined in the first syllable of Elgol.

Glen Scaladal

This short, wild glen sandwiched between Beinn Leacach and Ben Meabost possesses an amazing feeling of remoteness, and is rarely visited by walkers. The ruins of a few buildings suggest that the glen was once inhabited, but there is little of contemporary record that expands on this. As an escape route from Cladach a'Ghlinne to Kilmarie, it is useful, once you can locate the path.

The path begins where the shingle ends and keeps to the south side of the glen, moving well away from Scaladal Burn as it climbs higher into a wide corrie on the north-western flank of Ben Meabost. Although unbroken, the path frequently becomes vague among the tangle of heather and tussock grass.

Towards the head of the glen, the burn divides, but at this stage you should be well above it, and heading for a fence (shown on OS maps), topped with barbed wire, beyond which an even wetter stretch of contouring leads into a gradual descent to gain the Kilmarie track, reaching it at the Robostan woodland, and not far from the road.

WALK 2.18:
Suidhe Biorach
(Prince Charles' Cave)

There are at least four places on Skye that bear the name 'Prince's Cave', alluding to their use as a shelter by Prince Charles Edward

Stuart (Bonnie Prince Charlie) on his flight across Skye in 1746, following his defeat at Culloden.

Tracing the Prince's route across Skye has become a vexed, and probably irresolvable, question in the eyes of academics. Everyone agrees, however, that it was from a cave at the southernmost tip of the Strathaird peninsula, near Suidhe Biorach, that after a stay of six days (having landed in Kilbride Bay on Sunday 29 June), the Prince left the shores of Skye on the evening of Friday 4 July 1746, bound for the mainland of Scotland, and France, never to return to Skye.

This walk to visit the cave takes in some splendid cliff scenery, but a visit to the cave is only advisable at low tide. The sea cliffs around Suibhe Biorach, are host to many sea-going birds, so it is best to avoid this walk during the breeding season, when the birds can behave aggressively.

Start/Finish: Elgol.
Distance: 2½km (1½ miles).
Ascent: Negligible.

Set off from the Elgol jetty, and head south above the beach, where you will find a path rising on to the cliff top, and then running on to Suidhe Biorach. The cliff top is a fascinating, and a little hazardous, place to explore, fractured by mini geos and creeks.

The name Suidhe Biorach means Pointed Seat, and derives from the custom of childless women to sit there, hoping to end their infertility.

The cave in which Prince Charles sheltered lies a short way further on, close by a shoreline rock platform on the west side of the neat bay, Port an Luig Mhòir. Go beyond the rock platform, then descend to the shore, and return along the base of the cliffs to locate the cave, which is easily missed. It is a large through cave, filled with water (as a rule).

WALK 2.19:
Rubha na h-Easgainne

The southernmost tip of the Strathaird peninsula, Rubha na h-Easgainne, is, as a climax to a walk, a little disappointing, ending in a sprawl of bogginess that only a geographical purist would want to visit. Thankfully, the journey, which I have made six times now (always in glorious weather, when I should have been somewhere else, taking photographs), is a far better proposition than the arrival, and enjoys a fine tramp along quiet lanes and old tracks, through isolated villages, and always with views of Loch Slapin, Loch Eishort and the low ground of Sleat to draw the eye.

Whether you continue all the way to Rubha na h-Easgainne is almost unimportant, but, by way of encouragement, this remote spot is a fine spot for quiet contemplation, from which, welded among the rocks, you can spy upon the true inhabitants of these coastal margins, the birdlife, the seals and the otters.

> **Start:** Kilmarie. Roadside parking at GR.545172.
> **Finish:** Glasnakille. GR.537131. Unless retracing your steps, transport will be needed at each end.
> **Distance:** 8km (5 miles), between Kilmarie and Glasnakille, plus 4km (2½ miles) in total, to continue to Rubha na h-Easgainne and back.
> **Ascent:** 150m (490 feet).

From the roadside parking, opposite the Camasunary track, turn right and go down the road, until you reach the minor road that leads to Kilmarie House (GR.553173).

The road leads to a small bay where the Abhainn Cille Mhaire flows into the sea. Nearby is the old graveyard, as Otta Swire describes: "...strange, unexpected, and rather desolate, with the pebbles of the seashore reaching to its gates. It has been planted with yew and cypress; purple flags and red-hot pokers bloom among the graves, giving it a charm unique among Skye burial-grounds".

Crowning a rocky headland opposite stand the remains of Dun

Ringill, the stronghold of the MacKinnons before they evacuated to Caisteal Maol, and, for the curious, this can be reached by a bridge across the Abhainn Cille Mhaire near Kilmarie House, through woodlands to follow the coastline to the dun, one side of which is formed by the sea cliff, though the entrance is from the landward side.

The roadway continues past Kilmarie House and the burial ground to a group of cottages, where you move away from the shoreline to pursue an old track linking with the road end at Drinan, then climbing above wooded cliffs to meet another road reaching out from the Broadford-Elgol road.

The on-going track continues past Dun Liath, crosses a burn and continues to reach the road end at Glasnakille. From there it presses on, past Spar Cave (see Walk 2.20) and Dun Grugaig, to within about ½km (600 yards) or so of Rubha na h-Easgainne, to which the intrepid and the curious will continue. Less adventurous souls will elect to visit Spar Cave instead, before worrying about transport and how to get back.

Kilmarie church

The site of the old church at Kilmarie is no longer evident, its final remains having been swept away by the sea during a severe storm in the 1920s. Legend has it that the storm followed the burial near the old church of an unknown sailor, taken from the sea. According to an old Gaelic verse "the sea will search the four russet divisions of the universe to find her children", which supports the view that a body taken from the sea should always be buried near the water's edge, or the sea, in seeking to recover its own, will devastate the land in search of it.

The Kilmarie church is said to have stood on the site of the ancient church of St Maelruba, the patron saint of central and southern Skye, and a follower of St Columba's teaching.

WALK 2.20:
Spar Cave

Some would argue that the splendour of Strathaird is its Spar Cave, on the east side of the peninsula, not far from Rubha na h-Easgainne. In Walter Scott's The Lord of the Isles, *this is the "...mermaid's alabaster grot" of which Allan is dreaming moments before he is murdered: "And o'er his head the dazzling spars, Gleam like a firmament of stars".*

In his Journal, *Scott describes "a splendid gallery, adorned with the most dazzling crystallisations, [that] descends with rapidity to the brink of a pool, of the most limpid water". This was certainly one of the sights of Skye during Scott's day, but many of its loveliest "spars" were stolen as souvenirs.*

The cave was formed when a basaltic dyke was eroded by wave action to form a deep cleft, and was frequently visited during the nineteenth century. It is only accessible for a short period each day, when the tide is low.

If you do venture into the cave, please take away only memories, and treat this unique masterpiece rather more considerately than your nineteenth-century counterparts.

Start/Finish: Glasnakille. GR.537131.
Distance and Ascent: Nominal: allow 1½ hours, but keep an eye on the tide.

At the T-junction in Glasnakille, turn right, and continue a short way to a byre, beyond which a gap in a fence lets you access a path that descends to the edge of shoreline cliffs. The way down to a rocky inlet is not immediately obvious, but once traced and the shoreline reached, go left beneath the cliffs to the next headland. A short bout of slippery seashore rock ledges and seaweed soon brings you to the entrance to the cave. Note that this stretch can only be negotiated at low tide.

A torch will be needed to effect any exploration; the floor is dappled with tiny pools, and at one point rises steeply before slipping down to a deep pool, across which one of Scott's sailors swam. The cave ends a short way beyond the pool.

Walls encrusted in calcium carbonate reflect the torchlight, and give the cave a truly magical appeal, Scott's "enchanted cell".

Spar Cave

In Gaelic the cave is called Slochd Altrimen, the Cave of the Nursling, which commemorates a tale from the ninth century. Once, when the Lords of Skye were away fighting, the King of Ulster attacked the Hebrides and carried off Colonsay's son as a hostage. On returning from the inevitable revenge trip, the ship was wrecked in Loch Slapin, and the young Colonsay only saved by the speedy intervention of a Skye princess, Dounhuila, who sent people to rescue him. Alas, her father and his were at odds, and so young Colonsay spent his time imprisoned in Dun Glass. Dounhuila, however, fell in love with him, and bore him a child, which she entrusted a servant to keep in the Spar Cave, visiting only to nurse the child. Colonsay's dog, also saved in the shipwreck, was their guardian against wild beasts and outside interference, that, and a web of tales about a haunted cave where mermaids sang and drove men mad.

In time, Dounhuila helped Colonsay to escape, and he succeeded in bringing peace to the two families, ratifying the peace by his marriage to Dounhuila.

SECTION 3:
Minginish

Minginish (pronounced with a hard 'g') is that central-west wedge of land confined by Loch Scavaig in the south and Loch Bracadale in the north. It is best known for the Cuillin, to which everyone beats a trail sooner or later. But Minginish, north of Loch Brittle, has walking opportunity amid wild tracts of remote coastline and moorland as serious and as enjoyable as any visit to the Cuillin.

The Cuillin

The Cuillin not surprisingly are a Mecca for rock climbers and mountain walkers who feel comfortable and secure on steep rock in exposed places. Here there is more exposed rock and more precarious situations than any other single range of mountains in Britain. It is no place, however, for novices, while even those with experience on many of the mainland peaks will find situations that intimidate and circumstances that make nonsense of everything that applies elsewhere, for the Cuillin are a law unto themselves.

The name of the range has been spelt in many different ways, so it is hardly surprising that its origin is obscure. The current consensus is that it derives from the Norse word, *kjölen*, meaning 'high rocks'. Likewise, the name needs no suffix — hills — simply 'The Cuillin' is enough.

The main ridge is 12km (7½ miles) in length, and incorporates more than thirty major peaks, including eleven Munros and nine Tops. But anyone who might be tempted to think of this as a straightforward 7½ mile walk is in for a catalogue of surprises. Not least among these is the fact that many of the rocks are magnetic, and render a compass unreliable. Added to which the ridge is anything but a direct line, and pursues a convoluted course not only laterally but in its countless undulations. There are whole sections of the ridge, indeed the greater part of it, where 'walking' is impossible, where sheer and exposed rock barriers halt further pedestrian progress.

Although a trifle prone to the over-dramatisation of landscapes rife among early writers, H V Morton, who ventured *In Search of Scotland* in the 1920s — quite late in terms of the exploration of the Cuillin, though he was not a mountaineer — did nevertheless capture the essence of the range as seen by visitors for the first time. "Imagine", he wrote, "Wagner's 'Ride of the Valkyries' frozen in stone and hung up like a colossal screen against the sky. It seems as if Nature when she hurled the Coolins up into the light of the sun said: 'I will make mountains which shall be the essence of all that can be terrible in mountains. I will pack into them all the fearful mystery of high places. I will carve them into a million queer, horrible shapes. Their scarred ravines, on which nothing shall grow, shall lead up to towering spires of rock, sharp splinters shall strike the sky along their mighty summits, and they shall be formed of rock unlike any other rock so that they will never look the same for very long, now blue, now grey, now silver, sometimes seeming to retreat or to advance, but always drenched in mystery and terrors.'"

Non-scrambling walkers coming to Skye for the first time might be forgiven for supposing that the Cuillin are a totally forbidden territory, for so it seems. Substantially, this is true. No inexperienced walker should even think about venturing among the Cuillin, for they will present problems and difficulties that ought more properly to be addressed first in less hazardous situations elsewhere. Nor should anyone contemplate exploring the range in less than ideal weather conditions; any notions of sitting out a passing rain storm or the swirling mists that suddenly appear should be banished instantly; it is not unknown for the Cuillin to remain shrouded and rain-drenched for weeks at a time.

Yet sensible walkers, who heed the advice that all writers about the Cuillin proffer, do not have to forgo completely the magnificent walking the range offers. Always with an eye to the weather and with the care the range demands, the walks in this book will provide more than ample satisfaction. None, not even the easiest, is easy: all of them require constant vigilance. The parts of the Cuillin that involve scrambling ability, beyond one or two simple moves, do not feature in the book, but walkers should be fit and healthy and accustomed to the strenuous levels of activity that regular British hill-walking demands.

The dividing line between a scramble and a walk is a simple one —

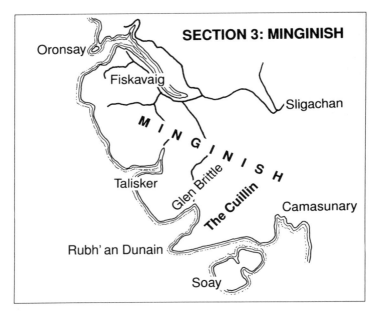

it is the point at which you need hands to aid progress, rather than merely for balance.

Walkers who, having tasted what the Cuillin have to offer, want to develop their skills and experience in a controlled and supervised way, should seriously consider enlisting the support of a guide (see 'Useful Information and Addresses').

Glen Sligachan

This remarkable glen, by far the finest on Skye, forms the eastern boundary of Minginish, and separates the Cuillin from Strathaird. For walkers it is an ideal place to become familiar with Skye terrain, and the sort of difficulties it presents. The complete walk from Sligachan to Camasunary or Elgol is, for anyone, a magnificent proposition. The path through the glen serves to allow walkers an insight into Harta and Lota Corries, and to access Loch Coruisk in less than hazardous circumstances. But the distances through the glen should not be underestimated, and the going can at times be very trying.

Loch Brittle to Loch Bracadale

The vast area north of Loch Brittle, across Loch Eynort and up to the southern shores of Loch Bracadale, is infrequently visited, and forms a massive moorland region, far less demanding than the rest of Minginish, but a long way from assistance if help is needed. North of Loch Brittle the first great sea cliffs are encountered, though many of them are crumbling and represent a danger best avoided. Here, too, lies Glen Brittle Forest and a cross-country route to Loch Eynort. Both offer easier walking.

Glen Eynort has none of the dramatic scenery of its neighbours, and forms a largely grassy oasis, a green and peaceful corner of Minginish, described by an early nineteenth-century writer (Sarah Murray) as "silent and forlorn as an uninhabited island".

It is possible to walk from Glen Eynort to Talisker Bay, following the coastline for much of the way, but this traverses very steep grassy slopes above sharp-edged cliffs and a prolonged tussle with rough moorland, all of it a long way from outside assistance in an emergency.

For a taste of the Minginish coastline without the trauma of the Eynort-Talisker option, the stretch that leads north to Fiskavaig is far more acceptable, and has an unmistakable escape route never more than a mile away, due east. Talisker Bay itself is a fascinating place to explore. From Talisker House you take a broad track down to the beach from where you can see the dramatic stacks off Talisker Point.

WALK 3.1:
[Sgurr nan Gillean]

Of all the images of Skye perhaps that of Sgurr nan Gillean and its adjacent peaks viewed from the vicinity of Sligachan is the most instantly recognisable, a vision of ruggedness and challenge. And challenging it is, too, for walkers without scrambling ability simply cannot reach its summit, but, providing they call a halt before the nerves start twitching, they can make a splendid and adventurous day out of trying.

Certain it is that this inaccessibility should not be the reason to avoid Sgurr nan Gillean: the walk round to the South East Ridge is quite outstanding, with consistently good views, especially of Bla Bheinn, and at least one of the two summits described in Walk 3.2 will provide ample compensation.

Start/Finish: Sligachan. GR.487299.
Distance: Depends on ability. About 12km (7½ miles).
Ascent: 950m (3115 feet)(maximum).

Only a short way from the Sligachan Hotel a path leaves the Dunvegan road, aiming for Sgurr nan Gillean, and leads to a footbridge spanning the Allt Dearg Mór. Flattish moorland lies beyond, with the path rising gently to reach the Allt Dearg Beag. An array of small cascades and inviting pools leads to a higher footbridge, where the path divides.

Cross the bridge, and stay with the ensuing path, past Nead na h-Iolaire into Coire Riabhach where a tiny lochan lies amid a spread of heather and rock. Traversing the bowl of the corrie high above the lochan, the path climbs around Sgurr nan Gillean's east face, ascending steep rocky slopes and passing beneath the towering Pinnacle Ridge gradually to climb out of the corrie.

As the path moves into a smaller corrie, a mess of crags and fallen rocks, it becomes less obvious, but is cairned to the gully at the rear of the corrie and across the spread of boulders below the South East Ridge, finally gaining the skyline midway between Sgurr nan Gillean and Sgurr Beag.

Non-scramblers can, with satisfaction, call a halt at this point, though they can go a little further yet. The South East Ridge has a number of evident ways on to it, but the higher you climb the harder does the going become, sooner or later calling into play one's sense of what is comfortable and what is not. **It is stressed that no one should be tempted here to extend the limits of their experience.**

With care, most walkers can get within a tantalising and infuriating 30m (less than 100 feet) of the summit, but what remains is narrow and extremely exposed, and leads to a spectacular summit from which none of the adjoining ridges is visible: this strange sense of isolation can be very intimidating, and is best left to those with a good head for heights.

Do not go up what you might not climb down. However high you climb, the only return for walkers is back the way you came.

WALK 3.2:
Sgurr Beag
[and Sgurr na h-Uamha]

Although lying south of Sgurr nan Gillean and other Cuillin peaks, Sgurr Beag and Sgurr na h-Uamha are effectively the last nails in the Cuillin Horseshoe. Few walkers single out these summits for individual attention, most visitors simply adding them to their day's tally only after tackling Sgurr nan Gillean. A rather higher proportion of walkers decide to visit them having failed to reach the top of Gillean, although Sgurr na h-Uamha is certainly no easier to conquer.

Those who recognise their limits, however, will find much satisfaction in making Sgurr Beag the express object of their attention, and from it gain a fine view of Sgurr nan Gillean's South East Ridge. The continuation to conical Sgurr na h-Uamha, perched above Lota Corrie, while certain to be beyond anyone without good scrambling ability, nevertheless will withstand a little prodding, providing it is not taken too far.

Start/Finish: Sligachan. GR.487299.
Distance: Depends on ability. About 12km (7½ miles).
Ascent: Sgurr Beag 750m (2460 feet); Sgurr na h-Uamha (maximum) 980m (3215 feet) — assuming a return over Sgurr Beag.

Walk 3.1 should be followed from Sligachan to the foot of Sgurr nan Gillean's South East Ridge, from where the rocky top of Sgurr Beag is only a short distance away in a south-easterly direction, its highest point directly above a neat corrie that plunges to Glen Sligachan below.

An easy slope, mostly grass and rock, drops to Bealach a'Ghlas-choire, from where it is possible to descend south of east into Glen Sligachan. Anyone returning to Sligachan by this route will need to ford the glen river before reaching the main glen path. From the bealach you can also descend scree and rough ground into Lota Corrie and down to Harta Corrie for a wild and rugged exploration of these fine Cuillin corries (see Walk 3.19).

[The continuation to Sgurr na h-Uamha requires good scrambling ability, and though the first of its two sections may be found to be comparatively easy, the upper part has a number of difficulties that have to be reversed by anyone successfully getting beyond them. **Without confidence and ability in such situations you are advised not to attempt Sgurr na h-Uamha.**]

WALK 3.3:
Coire a'Bhasteir [Am Basteir]

Am Basteir cannot be ascended by walkers lacking scrambling ability; even the easiest line involves a tricky descent on the ascent that turns back many an ambition. An exploration of the secluded Coire a'Bhasteir, is more than adequate compensation, however, and leads to a sheltered lochan surrounded by scree slopes and towering peaks.

Start/Finish: Sligachan. GR.487299.
Distance: (Loch a'Bhasteir) 10km (6¼ miles).
Ascent: (Loch a'Bhasteir) 590m (1935 feet).

Follow Walk 3.1 as far as the second footbridge (across the Allt Dearg Beag). Do not cross the bridge, but continue along the river's true left bank ascending towards the conspicuous and impressive Coire a'Bhasteir gorge. The rock walls of the gorge merge with rock slabs at the base of Sgurr a'Bhasteir, through which a route is cairned, cutting across the North East Ridge of Sgurr a'Bhasteir. There are a couple of moments where the use of hands will be needed, but the emphasis should be on keeping to the line of cairns. More cairns lead on beyond the top of the gorge into the corrie and its lochan. Walkers should return from this point.

The cliffs of Am Basteir rise at the back of the corrie above scree and boulder slopes up which lies the route to Bealach a'Bhasteir, the key to the east ridge of Am Basteir. [Although the east ridge involves little more than walking or easy scrambling, a short section about two-thirds of the way up on polished holds necessitates a 3m (10 feet) descent, facing inwards. This will halt anyone without scrambling ability, and has to be renegotiated on the return.]

Coire a'Bhasteir

Well seen from Sligachan, Coire a'Bhasteir is hemmed in by the most distinctive of Cuillin skylines stemming from Sgurr nan Gillean, on the left, across Am Basteir and its prominent 'tooth' to the far more accessible Sgurr a'Bhasteir on the right.

At the heart of the corrie, Loch a'Bhasteir feeds the infant Allt Dearg Beag, soon to be sent on its way through the Basteir Gorge. Shaded from the sun for much of the year, Coire a'Bhasteir has an air of dark power and secrecy, promoted also by the difficulty of its approaches – as Seton Gordon describes in The Charm of Skye, *"...there are days... when the Cuillin are alive with benign spiritual forces; when the hill silence tells of many wonderful things; when hill, sky, and ocean glow with life and energy". Such feelings do flow from the Cuillin, adding a dimension that the receptive, willingly or otherwise, will perceive. Secluded Coire a'Bhasteir is well calculated to inspire such feelings, though a halt beside its lochan, a bite to eat and a drink produces just as ably sensations of satisfaction and well-being.*

At the back of the corrie, Bealach a'Bhasteir is one of two points of access to the main ridge, the other being Bealach nan Lice. Both are reached across steep boulders and scree, above which the path divides, left to reach Bealach a'Bhasteir, and right to follow a scree path below Am Basteir to the western end of Basteir Tooth, beyond which the path follows the base of a ridge to reach Bealach nan Lice.

WALK 3.4:
Sgurr a'Bhasteir

Lacking Munro status, and projecting northwards, away from the main Cuillin ridge, Sgurr a'Bhasteir seems an unlikely contender for a walker's attention, yet the view it provides of the Pinnacle Ridge of Sgurr nan Gillean is second to none, and more than compensates for anything it (debatably) lacks in other respects. Indeed, its fractured crest is the fine culmination to a couple of enjoyable approach ridges, and could be used as a preface to a circuit that goes on to gather Bruach na Frithe.

Start/Finish: Sligachan. GR.487299.
Distance: 11km (7 miles).
Ascent: 885m (2905 feet).

The route into Coire a'Bhasteir (Walk 3.3) is the key to the ascent of Sgurr a'Bhasteir, and leads you to a choice of ascents, one by the North East Ridge, the other by the North West. Both ridges give pleasant walking, with scrambling of the very easiest kind.

If heading for the North East Ridge, follow the route through the Coire a'Bhasteir gorge until you are beyond the slabby section above the gorge. Then divert, right, to gain the ridge, and follow it to the summit.

Am Basteir and the Basteir Tooth from Bealach nan Lice

The approach by the North West Ridge leaves Walk 3.3 below the gorge and climbs to the obvious bealach between Sgurr a'Bhasteir and its northerly companion, Meall Odhar, from where the summit may easily be reached.

Return by the same route, or continue southwards to approach the main Cuillin ridge, branching slightly right towards the Bealach nan Lice, and returning through Fionn Choire on a good path (see Walk 3.5).

WALK 3.5:
Fionn Choire, Bealach Nan Lice [and Sgurr a'Fionn Choire]

"The green and pleasant Fionn Choire was flooded in sunlight, and as I climbed (over ground carpeted with bright flowers) an unsurpassed view north and west gradually unfolded itself...At the head of the [corrie] was a vast silence, broken only by the drip of a small burn over steel-blue stones. Motionless above the corrie a dark cloud floated. Here was shade; all around was sun-flood, so that the eye looked from darkness to light — the soft mellow sunlight of western seas that speak so strongly to those who understand their message." (*Seton Gordon*, The Charm of Skye)

Seton Gordon's "vast silence" may now be broken by more than dripping water, for Fionn Choire (the Fair Corrie) provides access to one of the easiest passes across the main Cuillin ridge, the Bealach nan Lice, and to one of the easiest (a relative term) of the ridge summits, Bruach na Frithe. Now, amid the silence, you will hear echoing chatter and the clatter of slithering rocks put in motion by walkers' feet.

Unlike most Cuillin corries, Fionn Choire is both broad and grassy, and in itself offers an enjoyable and satisfying walk without the necessity of pushing on to bag a summit.

Above the corrie, the Bealach nan Lice crosses the main ridge and drops by a stone shoot into the upper reaches of Lota Corrie. [From close by the bealach, a simple ascent, but one that requires easy scrambling ability, may be made of Sgurr a'Fionn Choire, a fine viewpoint for Am Basteir and its tooth.]

Start/Finish: Lay-by on Dunvegan road (A863), near access track to Alltdearg House. GR.479298.
Distance: Fionn Choire: 11km (7 miles).
Bealach nan Lice and Sgurr a'Fionn Choire: 12km (7½ miles).
Ascent: Fionn Choire: 650m (2135 feet).
Bealach nan Lice: 800m (2625 feet).
Sgurr a'Fionn Choire 885m (2905 feet).

Though less obviously a corrie than those that nestle beneath the crags of the Cuillin, the heathery, hummocky expanse of Coire na Circe spreads about the Allt Dearg Mór, and forms a traditional cross-country route between Sligachan and Glen Brittle, reached across the Bealach a'Mhaim. On any day, fair or foul, the walk beside the Allt Dearg Mór, with its many chattering cascades and bright-eyed pools, is a delight, and a perfectly adequate excursion for a lazy day.

Near the lay-by, a broad track (signposted: 'Footpath to Glen Brittle') leads in to Allt Dearg House. As the house is approached, leave the track and move right, on to a peaty path that for a short distance can prove messy after prolonged rain. This obstacle, however, is soon passed, and the on-going path improves with height, becoming a stony path on which good progress is made, though the river offers photographers many an excuse to frame a picture or two.

About 1km (½ mile) before the Bealach a'Mhaim, at a modest cairn, the path forks. Here, leave the main path, and go left shortly to cross the burn at an easy ford. Beyond, a clear path rises gradually, parallel with the Allt an Fhionn-choire, to enter the corrie. As it reaches the corrie rim, the burn appears in front of you, in a deep gully, easily crossed to enter the corrie above.

The onward path is cairned, but not clearly so. Bealach nan Lice lies at the head of the corrie, to the left, with a stony path rising to it. Head in this direction. If going no further than the corrie you have quite a sizeable arena to explore in which a few small lochans repose.

For the bealach, continue with the path, tending to the left, and rising to meet a bouldery, and then scree, path as the headwall of the corrie is approached. Paths, from Sgurr a'Bhasteir, arrive from the left, joining with the Fionn Choire path just below the bealach. The 'surprise' view of Lota Corrie from the bealach is outstanding, and, for those heading for Bruach na Frithe (Walk 3.6), improves with height.

[Sgurr a'Fionn Choire stands immediately to the west of the Bealach nan Lice, and is another splendid viewpoint. Its ascent requires a simple scramble of about 50m (150 feet), but keep well to the right of the steep cliffs flanking the bealach.]

WALK 3.6:
Bruach na Frithe

Any use of the term 'easy' in the context of the Cuillin is destined to misinterpretation, yet of all the Cuillin heights, Bruach na Frithe vies with Sgurr na Banachdich for the distinction of being the 'easiest' to ascend. And so it is, but the climb to this renowned viewpoint, popular as it is, remains an energetic exercise and potentially confusing in poor visibility. The first recorded ascent was in 1845, by Professor Forbes and Duncan MacIntyre.

The only approach that does not involve scrambling is that through Fionn Choire. With a little scrambling ability, and a head for heights, you could tackle the North West Ridge. Walkers tackling the Cuillin summits for the first time will find Bruach na Frithe ideal for the purpose. The bad news is that the rest are all more difficult.

Start/Finish: Lay-by on Dunvegan road (A863), near access track to Alltdearg House. GR.479298.
Distance: 13km (8 miles).
Ascent: 900m (2955 feet).

Follow Walk 3.5 to the Bealach nan Lice, and there traverse (right) below Sgurr a'Fionn Choire (on the Fionn Choire side), on a good path (take the higher of the two on offer) that leads to a shallow bealach between Sgurr a'Fionn Choire and Bruach na Frithe, where the rest of the main ridge springs into view. The ensuing East Ridge

The North West Ridge of Bruach na Frithe

of Bruach na Frithe is no more than a moderate walk, with a little optional scrambling en route. The view from the summit — the only Cuillin summit with a triangulation pillar — is one of the Cuillin's finest.

[The ascent of Bruach na Frithe's North West Ridge provides a rather more exhilarating route, and involves some exposed, but otherwise simple, scrambling towards the top. Furthermore, as in many areas of the Cuillin, the rock is basalt, and likely to be slippery when wet. The ridge is best reached by following Walk 3.5 until you start climbing up into Fionn Choire, and then leaving the path to ascend, half-right, to gain the lower part of the ridge — here formed as two broad spurs separated by the bleak corrie that houses the Allt Mor an Fhinn Choire. Alternatively, continue until, as you pursue the corrie path, you reach the gully through which the Allt an Fhionn-choire flows. Then go right across less steep ground to gain the north-east spur rather more directly.]

[Once the two spurs combine, so the scrambling begins. There is a rough path about 30m (100 feet) below the crest that avoids some of the scrambling, but this can be misleading if joined too low down the ridge.

If you want to see how you cope with a scrambling ascent for the first time, this is a good route on which to begin, but choose a dry and clear day.]

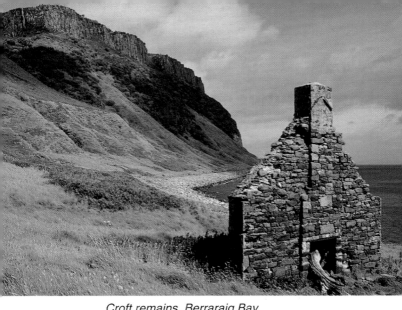

Croft remains, Berraraig Bay
The northern end of the Trotternish Ridge

The southern Duirinish coastline
Pinnacles of the Quiraing

[The Main Ridge: Bruach na Frithe to Sgurr a'Mhadaidh]

[Between Bruach na Frithe and Sgurr a'Mhadaidh the great expanse of Coire na Creiche (see Walk 3.7) rises to a spectacular traverse that, for walkers, is almost a total no-go area. The main Cuillin ridge here cavorts over Sgurr na Bhairnich, An Caisteal and Bidein Druim nan Ramh before moving on to Sgurr a'Mhadaidh.

This is not a section where anyone without scrambling ability should venture; indeed, there are sections where scramblers may need to raise their game to those that rock climbers play if they wish to proceed with confidence.]

[Sgurr na Bhairnich]

[The simplest way of reaching Sgurr na Bhairnich is to descend from Bruach na Frithe by its south ridge. This is an exhilarating proposition, and involves a little scrambling, notably on leaving the summit of Bruach na Frithe.]

[More conventionally it is ascended from Coir' a'Tairneilear either by way of a steep scree gully leading to a deep gap between Bhairnich and An Caisteal, visible from the corrie as a prominent notch on the skyline, and then by scree-covered ledges, or, rather more acceptably, by first taking in An Caisteal from the Bealach Harta.]

[Bealach Harta is the only 'easy' pass over the main ridge from Coir' a'Tairneilear, and is located right at the back of the corrie, just north-east of Bidein Druim nan Ramh. The name appears to be of uncertain origin: most books do call it Bealach Harta, but at least one other uses the name Bealach Coir' a'Tairneilear.]

[An Caisteal]

[The crossing of An Caisteal (not named on maps) is awkward and sensational, mostly on outward sloping slabs. The normal line of ascent is by its South West Ridge from Bealach Harta. By this route, from the bealach, a short steep wall leads to a level section of ridge and on to a much narrower section that involves striding courageously across a void where basaltic dykes across the ridge have weathered; another similar gap higher up can be avoided on rubbishy ledges.]

[Bidein Druim nan Ramh]

[Without moderate-difficult rock climbing skills, the three summits of Bidein Druim nan Ramh are inaccessible, with, almost predictably, the highest proving to be the most difficult to reach. The base of the summit rocks on the northern side provides the only by-pass for walkers, and at least enables a spectacular and precarious traverse to be made between the Bealach Harta and Bealach na Glaic Moire, the latter lying between Bidein Druim nan Ramh and Sgurr a'Mhadaidh.]

[Sgurr an Fheadain]

[Composed mainly of basalt, and therefore best avoided when wet, this pyramidic peak rises from Coire na Creiche (see Walk 3.7) in dramatic fashion, its face split by the deep gash of Waterpipe Gully, a classic Very Severe rock climb.]

[Scramblers can choose between a simple scramble up the South East Ridge, or something more sensational, The Spur, up the broad slabby buttress to the left of Waterpipe Gully. This is very exposed in places, but gives an outstanding scrambling route to the main ridge.]

[The Main Ridge: Sgurr a'Mhadaidh to Sgurr na Banachdich]

[Though less of a frustration for walkers than the preceding section of the main ridge, the stretch between Sgurr a'Mhadaidh and Sgurr na Banachdich still poses problems for anyone without the ability to scramble at a fairly high level. The section forms the headwall of Coire a'Ghreadaidh, and proves to be a fine scrambler's traverse, hard in places, but the corrie facilitates access to a number of peaks, and, in itself, provides a satisfying walk (see Walk 3.8).]

WALK 3.7:
Coire na Creiche

It is as the road into Glen Brittle crosses a broad watershed that the first full view is obtained of Coire na Creiche, an expansive, shallow corrie divided by Sgurr an Fheadain and its distinctive Waterpipe Gully into two upper corries, Coir' a'Tairneilear and Coir' a'Mhadaidh. It is a sudden and outstanding view that has enthralled visitors since the days when the road between Carbost and Glen Brittle was little more than a rough track.

Coir' a'Tairneilear is bounded on its north side by the North West Ridge of Bruach na Frithe and on its south by a subsidiary ridge extending from the main ridge (at Bidein Druim nan Ramh) to Sgurr an Fheadain. Coir' a'Mhadaidh is enclosed on its south side by the spur of Sgurr Thuilm, meeting the main ridge at Sgurr a'Mhadaidh. [NOTE: Old maps and books, notably the excellent 1923 edition of the map The Black Cuillin *produced by the Scottish Mountaineering Club, and Ben Humble's book,* The Cuillin of Skye *(and, no doubt, others) have these two upper corries the wrong way round.*]

Walkers without scrambling ability will find the main ridge across Coire na Creiche a most difficult section; even good scramblers will have moments of doubt where the self-preservation factor rises dramatically. Set against this impregnability, the corrie itself provides two excellent walks, often accessible and worthwhile when the tops are shrouded in mist. One tours the corrie at a fairly high level, but is generally undemanding and on well-defined pathways most of the way. The second walk visits a fascinating series of waterfalls, gorges and pools, known as the Fairy Pools.

3.7a: Coire na Creiche

Start/Finish: Forest picnic site. GR.423263.
Distance: 8½km (5¼ miles).
Ascent: 350m (1150 feet).

Leave the car park/picnic area and turn left down the road until you can drop to a burn and then reach the Sligachan path. Ignore the path descending to the River Brittle. Follow instead the path below the forest, climbing easily with good views into Coire na Creiche, and press on as far as the second cairn on the Bealach a'Mhaim, from where there is a fine view of the northern Cuillin peaks. For a slightly more elevated view, nearby Am Màm can be 'conquered' in a matter of minutes.

Cross a stony plateau, just below the bealach lochan, and follow, a well-established route used by the nineteenth-century pioneers of Cuillin climbing into Coire na Creiche around the North West Ridge of Bruach na Frithe. The path makes a steady descent to cross the Coir' a'Tairneilear burn. If you want to shorten the walk, or combine it with a visit to the Fairy Pools, this is the point of departure, descending with the Allt Coir' a'Tairneilear (keep to its true right bank).

Continue below Sgurr an Fheadain, and when two paths appear, take the higher one, to cross the base of Waterpipe Gully. The gully is the most outstanding in the Cuillin, and the first to be explored. Its 365m (1200 feet) were first ascended in September 1895, when it was described as "affording constant, interesting and sometimes difficult climbing" in a classic piece of unintentional understatement – other climbers later described some of its twenty-five pitches as "monstrous". It is still a severe undertaking. Gazing up at it, the pleasures of being a non-climber spring easily to mind.

Coire na Creiche

The path continues below Coir' a'Mhadaidh, and after crossing the descending burn, changes direction to run westwards with increasing obscurity that becomes total once beyond Sgurr Thuilm. A few cairns show some of the way forward across stretches of grass below scree.

As a large expanse of boulders is encountered, so the time comes to start descending the trackless moor, aiming for the river bend at GR.430257. Here, in all but the most abnormal conditions, you can step across a narrow ravine, and so gain a path that rises to the road. (If the step across the ravine is too daunting, or impossible, continue downstream to cross at the roadbridge (GR.417245), and walk back up the road.)

Conclude by a short uphill pull to the picnic area in the forest.

3.7b: Allt Coir' a'Mhadaidh and the Fairy Pools

Start/Finish: Forest picnic site. GR.423263.
Distance: 6km (4 miles)(maximum).
Ascent: 275m (900 feet)(maximum).

This out-and-back walk can be terminated at any time, but the plan should be to take your time and enjoy the enchanting falls and pools.

Start from the car park/picnic site as Walk 3.7a, and descend from the road, this time ignoring the Sligachan path, and dropping to the river, aiming roughly for a prominent boulder on the river bank. You will need to cross an intermediate burn on the way.

Follow the river past an old shieling to reach the first of many waterfalls. Beyond, the burn flows down a neat gorge, creating cascades and pools galore.

The 'Fairy Pools' are two pools close together, which can be reached, with care, from the bank. Here you will find a rock arch dividing the pools, and a perfect spot for lunch, midges permitting.

Continue along the burnside path, ascending towards Coir' a'Tairneilear, at the base of which you will meet the path described in Walk 3.7a. From here, either return the same way, or continue with the rougher section of that walk.

WALK 3.8:
Coire a'Ghreadaidh

Split by the lower crags and tops of Sgurr a'Ghreadaidh into two small upper corries, the great bowl of Coire a'Ghreadaidh is a worthy objective for a day's outing, and though often available when clouds cover the main ridge, the real beauty of this walk lies in its seaward views, across Loch Brittle to the island of Rhum.

Start/Finish: Glen Brittle Youth Hostel. GR.409225.
Distance: 6½km (4 miles).
Ascent: 385m (1265 feet).

Leave the road opposite the youth hostel for the true left bank of the Allt a'Choire Ghreadaidh, and in minutes reach a waterfall that sets the scene for the next kilometre (½ mile) or so. A fine gorge runs on, with a splendid display of cascades, embellished by outward views across Loch Brittle that are typical of many among the Cuillin. At one point the path, often wet and boggy, comes very close to the ravine, and care is needed for a while. As the ravine expires, so the path curves to expose the vastness of the corrie above, and when the Cuillin sun shines, there are fewer more inviting places.

The corrie headwall is formed by three huge mountains, all Munros, Sgurr a'Mhadaidh, Sgurr a'Ghreadaidh and Sgurr na Banachdich, while between the last two lies a smaller summit, Sgurr Thormaid.

Between the lower part of the corrie and the upper, rocky reaches lies a band of slabs down which the Allt a'Choire Ghreadaidh performs a series of waterslides. As you approach the base of the waterslides look for an indistinct path through heather on the right of the falls, and use this to rejoin the burn at the top.

[The upper corrie seems barren and inhospitable, as indeed it can be. The only way on to the main ridge lies in the top left of the corrie, via a gap called An Dorus, but from it progress for the non-scrambler in any direction is impossible.] With the benefit of height, the view across Glen Brittle, through the gap in the hills opposite (Bealach Brittle) extends to the Outer Isles.

Go back the same way, which will prove just as rewarding as the ascent.

WALK 3.9:
Sgurr Thuilm, [Sgurr a'Mhadaidh and Sgurr a'Ghreadaidh]

Sgurr Thuilm projects north-west from the main ridge which it meets at the southernmost, and highest, of the four tops that comprise Sgurr a'Mhadaidh. [Between the two, the connecting ridge requires scrambling ability at a fairly high standard, effectively putting Sgurr a'Mhadaidh out of bounds to walkers. An ascent can be made from An Dorus, said to be a historically important crossing point, much used during the times when the clans of the Island were at odds. This approach, though easier than that from Sgurr Thuilm, nevertheless involves moderate scrambling.]

[The traverse of all four tops of Sgurr a'Mhadaidh requires at least Moderate rock climbing skills, and involves some very exposed moves.]

[The ascent of Sgurr a'Ghreadaidh also uses An Dorus, and, as with Sgurr a'Mhadaidh, begins with a moderate scramble that sets the standard for what is to follow.]

Start/Finish: Glen Brittle Youth Hostel. GR.409225.
Distance: (Sgurr Thuilm only): 7½km (5 miles).
Ascent: 860m (2820 feet).

The only feasible approach for walkers to Sgurr Thuilm follows the true left bank of Allt a'Choire Ghreadaidh towards the flattened bowl of the corrie proper. As the entrance to the upper corrie is reached so the opportunities to cross the burn increase. Once across, Sgurr Thuilm is easily reached, up the rock and scree slopes of its western shoulder. About half way up a crag can be turned on the left, followed by more scree, before the West Ridge is reached, and followed to the summit — a shapely peak and a fine viewpoint.

103

By heading further into the corrie (see Walk 3.8), an ascent can be made from the waterslides, by a process of grass and scree slopes, targeting a saddle on the summit ridge above. This route will lengthen the walk slightly.

[Sgurr a'Mhadaidh]

[Only the highest top of this Munro overlooks Coire a'Ghreadaidh, and the easiest approach is from An Dorus – the prominent gap at the head of Coire an Dorus. The start from An Dorus is steep and awkward scrambling, but does lead to easier scrambling and loose boulder slopes that, on descent, can be confusing at the best of times, and especially so in mist.]

[Sgurr a'Ghreadaidh]

[Sgurr a'Ghreadaidh has two outstanding summits of almost equal height separated by a knife-edge linking ridge that is both hard and sensationally exposed. The ridge requires constant concentration and care. Since there is no easy approach to the South West Ridge, the customary ascent is by the north ridge, via An Dorus.]

WALK 3.10:
Sgurr na Banachdich
and Sgurr nan Gobhar

Vying with Bruach na Frithe for the distinction of being the easiest of the Cuillin Munros to reach, Sgurr na Banachdich nevertheless can be very confusing in mist and involves extensive negotiation of scree slopes. It lies about midway along the main Cuillin ridge, and is an excellent peak for newcomers to Cuillin wandering, one of the few 'weaknesses' in what must seem like an impregnable defence.

Of three possible lines of approach, only two are available to non-scramblers. One ascends through Coir'an Eich, while the other takes in the projecting ridge of conical Sgurr nan Gobhar. [There is an approach to Sgurr na Banachdich along the main ridge from Bealach Coire na Banachdich, but the crest of the ridge involves hard scrambling, while the variant, avoiding much of the difficulty, is potentially confusing.]

3.10a: Coir' an Eich route

Start/Finish: Glen Brittle Youth Hostel. GR.409225.
Distance: 7km (4.4 miles).
Ascent: 945m (3100 feet).

Coir' an Eich, recessed high beneath the slopes of Sgurr nan Gobhar and An Diallaid, offers the easiest and shortest approach available to walkers. Simple arithmetic, however, embracing the distance and ascent figures, should be enough to qualify the term 'easiest': as everywhere in the Cuillin, nothing is 'easy', everything involving hard collar work.

From the Glen Brittle road, set off along the true left bank of the Allt a'Choire a'Ghreadaidh to reach the burn descending from Coir' an Eich. Here leave the main corrie path and ascend beside the Coir' an Eich burn. The ascent, mainly of scree slopes, is hard work, but leads to a small corrie in a splendid situation.

Press on by crossing the burn and heading upwards – more scree – to gain the An Diallaid spur near its junction with the Sgurr nan Gobhar ridge. This takes the form of a small plateau, above which yet more stony slopes sporting a number of cairns lead to the broad-domed summit and surprisingly narrow crest of Sgurr na Banachdich.

For walkers, continuation in any direction is out of the question, but the spectacular views of the Cuillin ridge and Coruisk is more than ample reward for all the effort.

Just north of Sgurr na Banachdich lies Sgurr Thormaid, named after Professor Norman Collie, FRS, one of the pioneers of Cuillin exploration. Manchester-born Collie now lies buried in the old church-yard at Struan, next to his close friend and Cuillin explorer, John Mackenzie.

Walkers must return by the same route, but note that the descent can be confusing in poor visibility, complicated by a lack of promi-nent landmarks and a proliferation of cairns.

*The graves of Norman Collie and
John MacKenzie, Struan*

3.10b: Sgurr nan Gobhar route

Start/Finish: Glen Brittle Youth Hostel. GR.409225.
Distance: 7km (4.4 miles).
Ascent: 960m (3150 feet).

Between the starting point and the top of Sgurr nan Gobhar, there is little to support the view that the peak is worth the effort. The 'best' line follows the Allt a'Choire a'Ghreadaidh for a while, before branching away to tackle the 600m (2000 feet) scree spread of the south-west shoulder, keeping south of crags, to gain the summit.

The top of the mountain, however, proves to be a fine vantage point, and from it an excellent and narrow ridge — a mix of walking and easy scrambling — leads on to the small plateau at the junction with the An Diallaid spur. Here the above route is joined, and pursues one of a number of cairned routes up the stony slopes of Sgurr na Banachdich.

WALK 3.11:
Eas Mor and Coire na Banachdich

Eas Mor, the big waterfall, ranks among the finest on an island where cliffs, of one sort or another, and water are in plentiful supply. On this walk the waterfall is soon reached, but the route continues upwards, to explore the dark recesses of Coire na Banachdich. The walk simply climbs into the corrie, from which it then retreats, though it does provide the easiest approach to Sgurr Dearg.

Even without the intimacy that rock climbing breeds for the Cuillin summits, it is impossible not to be impressed by the primeval power of the landscape. Nor is that a hackneyed metaphor. Sweeping, barren slopes of crag and scree flow down into the corrie from the embracing ridges of Sgurr nan Gobhar and Sgurr na Banachdich. Bad weather simply reinforces the sensation, while brilliant sunshine spreads a mantle of well-being from the warmth of which you can look out on the hills that surround you, on the glistening seas and dark headlands, the hazy islands and far, blue mountains of the mainland.

Start/Finish: Glen Brittle memorial hut. GR.411216.
Distance: 4km (2½ miles).
Ascent: 390m (1280 feet).

From opposite the memorial hut the way into Coire na Banachdich angles up and right to cross the Allt Coire na Banachdich near a pipeline water supply to the farm. When the burn curves left, stay on the path, soon to reach the edge of the Eas Mor ravine. Just off the path a grassy platform provides a stunning view of the 25m (80 feet) falls, and this point alone makes a satisfying short walk.

Above the Eas Mor ravine, the path into Coire na Banachdich branches left, while that to the right heads across to Coire Lagan. Take the left fork and walk ahead on a boggy path that eases away from the burn to reach the top of a rise where the expanse of Coire na Banachdich springs into view. How far you continue up the ensuing path is a matter of choice. A short way on the path steepens and becomes rocky, and presses on into the back of the corrie.

WALK 3.12:
Sgurr Dearg
[and Inaccessible Pinnacle]

Of the three possible lines of ascent of Sgurr Dearg, only one is within the realms of walkers, and that climbs by way of the Bealach

Coire na Banachdich. [The alternative, and from Glen Brittle the obvious, approach by the West Ridge is more entertaining, but involves moderate scrambling, while the ascent by way of the An Stac screes calls for a level of stoicism not within the repertoire of sensible walking folk – the An Stac screes are best used in descent, or, even better, ignored altogether by walkers.]

[The Inaccessible Pinnacle, 'In Pin' to its devotees, is a bizarre appendage to Sgurr Dearg, a mighty wedge of rock anchored below the summit of the mountain, but contriving to overtop it by about 8m (25 feet). You can argue until the desert sands freeze whether a slender blade of rock stuck on the side of a mountain is the true summit of the mountain, but you will never persuade the Munroists that Sgurr Dearg should hold the distinction and not In Pin. As a result many a Munro-bagging ambition has been thwarted by In Pin, including Hugh Munro's.]

Even without the Inaccessible Pinnacle, Sgurr Dearg remains an impressive mountain, its summit a sharp arête in a most commanding position overlooking glaciated Coire Lagan and with outstanding seaward views.

Start/Finish: Glen Brittle memorial hut. GR.411216.
Distance: 7km (4.4 miles).
Ascent: 965m (3165 feet).

The path into Coire na Banachdich begins from the Glen Brittle hut, and climbs around sheep enclosures to the Allt Coire na Banachdich, which it crosses (at a water pipeline) to reach the true left bank. One of the beauties of this approach is that it soon reaches a spectacular gorge into which a great waterfall, Eas Mor, spills, a splendid sight, especially after rain.

As the head of the gorge is reached, so the path forks. Take the left branch, for a while staying close by the river, and then moving away to cross the broad base of the corrie. Most of the flanks of Coire na Banachdich form featureless slopes of scree, punctuated by crags. One such is Window Buttress, a spur rising to the West Ridge of Sgurr Dearg, around the base of which the path continues. Further on, the path reaches a deep-cut gorge below the corrie headwall, above which lies Bealach Coire na Banachdich, technically the easiest way between Glen Brittle and Coruisk, but still a demanding proposition.

At the foot of the headwall move right, towards Sgurr Dearg, to avoid crags high up at the back of the corrie, and following the main burn flowing into the gorge. A line of cairns leads up rocky slabs on the true left of the burn, where there is little or no scree with which to contend. Above the crags the route cuts back, and moves across to the bealach over a broad shelf that can be difficult to locate, on descent, in poor visibility.

From the bealach a cairned path leads up to the summit of Sgurr Dearg. The topography of Sgurr Dearg's summit is very confusing, caused by a rib of slabs that crosses the main Cuillin ridge at an angle not far from the top.

If mist threatens, this complexity, and the potential difficulty of finding the shelf below Bealach Coire na Banachdich, more than commends an early retreat. In favourable conditions, there is much to be said for settling comfortably on Sgurr Dearg's rocky top to watch the entertainment on In Pin.

[Inaccessible Pinnacle]

[This most difficult of the high summits of Britain, first ascended in 1880 by Charles and Lawrence Pilkington, is usually climbed by its East Ridge, a Moderate rock climb. Having done that, the conventional way off is an abseil down the shorter, more difficult, West Ridge. In favourable conditions, it is the enormous sense of exposure that proves more of a deterrent than the climb itself, which is mainly well-defined and makes use of many good, if polished, 'jug handles'.]

[Main Ridge: Sgurr Dearg to Sgurr Thearlaich]

[Between Sgurr Dearg and the top of the Great Stone Shoot leading to Sgurr Alasdair, the ridge above Coire Lagan is only accessible by those with good scrambling ability and, on some sections, rock climbing skills, too.

Here, alas, the walker must be content with a visit to splendid Coire Lagan (Walk 3.13), a prospect that will not disappoint.]

[Sgurr Mhic Choinnich]

[This fine, wedge-shaped peak overlooking Coire Lagan was named in honour of John Mackenzie, an early pioneer of exploration among the Cuillin, and close friend of Professor Norman Collie. Even the easiest line of ascent to Sgurr Mhic Choinnich, by the long north-west ridge from Bealach Coire Lagan, is a tough scramble, sensationally exposed, and which, other than for rock climbers, must be reversed, as there is no onward route beyond the summit.]

[Sgurr Thearlaich]

[Rising directly above the Great Stone Shoot, Sgurr Thearlaich, is named after Charles Pilkington who led the first ascent in 1884. The ascent involves rock climbing even on its easiest approach, from the top of the Great Stone Shoot.]

WALK 3.13:
Coire Lagan

All the corries of the Cuillin are dramatic and inspiring, but none more so than Coire Lagan, for here it is that non-scrambling walkers can safely view some of the "million queer, horrible shapes...scarred ravines...towering spires of rock" and "sharp splinters [that] strike the sky" described by H V Morton whilst In Search of Scotland.

For the walker there is no escape from the corrie, only retreat. Those that use this way, the only way, to ascend to the highest of the Cuillin, Sgurr Alasdair (Walk 3.14), have no choice but to retrace their steps, many of which will have been spent on the massive scree run of the Great Stone Shoot, an awesome sight, and an even more awesome experience.

But if you can content yourself with brooding majesty, a close acquaintance with the evidence of Creation on a cataclysmic scale, and a grandstand view of the antics of others, then there is no better place; Coire Lagan is superb, straightforward, and deservedly popular. Set in its midst a bijou lochan, iridescent, clear-watered, surrounded by glacier-planed boiler-plate slabs, lies cradled by encircling walls across which climbers trace their intrepid way with trivial importance. It is the perfect objective.

Whether you seek an excuse never to set foot on the high Cuillin, or the courage and inspiration to begin, this is the place to visit, and it serves both needs.

Start/Finish: Glen Brittle campsite. GR.414204.
Distance: 6½km (4 miles).
Ascent: 570m (1870 feet).

Cross the fence behind the campsite toilet block and ascend the path directly ahead, ignoring other paths right or left. Very soon a broad track is reached and crossed, as the path into the corrie eases upwards.

Further on a burn and path are reached that lead into Coir' a'Ghrunnda. Ignore this and press on upburn until the edge of the upper moor is reached where the going underfoot gives way to rock. Another branch path on the right shoots off to the climbers' playground of Sron na Ciche. This, too, is ignored, and the path pursued beneath the slopes of Sgurr Dearg, finishing steeply not far from the lochan.

Ahead is the towering cliff of Sgurr Mhic Choinnich, and, to its right, the massive runnel of scree that is the Great Stone Shoot. Overhead, or so it seems, loom Sgurr Alasdair and its nearer sibling, the mighty crag, Sron na Ciche.

WALK 3.14:
Sgurr Alasdair

This, the highest peak of the Cuillin, is sought after by everyone. It is a splendid, shapely mountain, with unrivalled views of silvered sea and floating blue-hazed islands, of crag and corrie, loch and burn, while on a good day you can see as far as Ben Nevis, 80km (50 miles) distant, and beyond.

For the walker it would be a disaster if this pinnacle of the Cuillin were denied to them, but thankfully, though Alasdair does not yield its supremacy with ease, a way can be found to its airy summit. As with other Cuillin peaks to which a walker might ascend, to describe the ascent of Sgurr Alasdair as a 'walk' involves a fair amount of elasticity in translation; some hand-work, good balance and a head for heights are all needed as the summit is approached.

Sgurr Alasdair is named after Alexander Nicolson, a Skye man, an early explorer, and the first man to climb the peak, in 1873, something he accomplished having already climbed Sgurr na Banachdich, crossed Sgurr Dearg, and descended into Coire Lagan, then to toil up the Great Stone Shoot, to conquer the highest of the Cuillin peaks. It was not until 1888, however, that Sgurr Alasdair was confirmed as the highest peak, and not, as contemporary map-makers thought, Sgurr Dearg.

Sgurr Alasdair does not lie on the main Cuillin ridge, but a little off to one side; it is the first of three summits on a ridge running south-west, over Sgurr Sgumain to Sron na Ciche, a ridge which it is generally considered provides the finest rock climbing in the Cuillin. That the summit lies just off the main ridge or at the start of a fine subsidiary ridge is, for walkers, immaterial, since without rock climbing and scrambling skills of a high order, continuation in any direction is out of the question; only a retreat, down the Great Stone Shoot, is feasible.

Start/Finish: Glen Brittle campsite. GR. 414204.
Distance: 8km (5 miles).
Ascent: 990m (3245 feet).

The ascent into Coire Lagan begins from the campsite at the head of Loch Brittle, by stepping over a fence behind the toilet block, beyond which a stony path heads straight up into the corrie. Almost immediately it is cut by a broad track running out towards Rubh' an Dùnain, but the route into Coire Lagan cannot be mistaken. Further on, the path divides as it reaches a burn. Keep left here; the alternative path crosses into Coir' a'Ghrunnda.

Continue up across the moor and into a lower corrie, where rock takes over underfoot, in due course to arrive at the lochan.

The Great Stone Shoot begins at the back of the corrie and is perfectly evident in good visibility. The lower section is composed of scree of all sizes, but the upper reaches have been worn bare, and require care. If the conditions are poor, finding the correct line up the scree can be difficult, and any attempt to do so avoided, there being a strong tendency to move too far to the right, on to Sgurr Sgumain.

Not by any stretch of imagination can the ascent of the stone shoot be called pleasurable; it represents a corner of Purgatory set aside for hard-line masochists, but it is the only way walkers will reach the top of Sgurr Alasdair.

At the top of the stone shoot turn right for a short and airy final pull up a narrow ridge to the neat summit. If you are blessed with the fairest of days, every agonising step up the stone shoot will be doubly rewarded.

Return by the same route only.

WALK 3.15:
Coir' a'Ghrunnda
[and Loch Coir' a'Ghrunnda]

Impressively rocky, wild, beautiful, and by far one of the finest glaciated corries on Skye, Coir' a'Ghrunnda lies within the arms of the continuing main Cuillin ridge, along which lie Sgurr Dubh Da Bheinn and Sgurr nan Eag, and the subsidiary ridge that contains Sgurr Alasdair, Sgurr Sgumain and Sron na Ciche. The scenery in the upper sanctuary is outstanding, where massive 'flows' of glaciated boiler-plate slabs contrast with clinically clean crags that soar skywards.

Like neighbouring Coire Lagan there is a stunning, sensational atmosphere about the place. The upper reaches are protected by a prominent rock band, above which reposes Loch Coir' a'Ghrunnda. For Seton Gordon "The symmetrical basin of Coire a'Ghrunnda lies behind steep, rocky slopes; there is just sufficient difficulty in climbing the approaches to the corrie to give a feeling of satisfaction when the climber reaches the loch".

[The loch itself is the highest expanse of water in the Cuillin, and the lack of attention it receives compared with its counterpart in Coire

Lagan lends greater appeal. The final part of the ascent to the loch involves some scrambling in a steep rock gully, and should not be undertaken in poor visibility, when route-finding is a problem, both ascending and descending. The approach across the lower moor is boggy, and the entrance to the corrie higher than imagined.]

Start/Finish: Glen Brittle campsite. GR.414204.
Distance: 10km (6¼ miles)(maximum).
Ascent: 700m (2300 feet)(maximum).

From the campsite follow the Coire Lagan path on to the moor as far as the first burn, then leave it, cross the burn, and follow a continuing path across the moor to the Allt Coire Lagan. Soon the path traverses a grassy hollow and continues to a prominent splintered rock. Here leave the main path – used by some to 'walk' round to Coruisk, though it is far from a walk and leads to all manner of confusion and risk beyond Gars-bheinn – and fork left.

Before long, branch left again and climb steeply to reach a traversing path – the original Coir' a'Ghrunnda path – arriving from Coire Lagan. Follow this, and after climbing past the base of Sron na Ciche begin a steep pull up a gully below a rock battlement on the left. As you ascend so the view into the corrie is revealed, an inspiring moment. Seaward there is a stunning view across Soay to the islands of Rhum and Eigg.

It is from this point that non-scramblers may wish to return, though they can continue a little way further yet.

[Loch Coir' a'Ghrunnda]

[Above you the burn issuing from the hidden lochan can be seen. A cairned path crosses a rocky shelf between cliffs (on the left) and the massive glaciated slabs for which the corrie is renowned, on the right. Note that at no time on the ascent do you cross the burn.]

[The path rises through scree to the base of the south side of Sron na Ciche, and teases its way through a massive boulder field, keeping slabs to the right. A rocky slope leads up to the final wave of slabs, passed by ascending a steep rocky gully (simple scrambling; awkward in reverse and when wet) to the left of the burn, which here is itself almost vertical. Once up the gully, a line of cairns leads the way to the lochan. Be sure to follow the cairns at the start of the descent, to avoid being drawn by the burn towards crags.]

WALK 3.16:
[The South Cuillin Ridge]

[Walkers who are defeated by the final scrambling section of the ascent to Coire a'Ghrunnda can pursue no further interest in the southernmost section of the Cuillin ridge. Those who can will be faced with more of the same, or harder, though there are a few weaknesses that will allow the intrepid to probe the ridge above the corrie. Any such exploration by non-scramblers, however, should be tempered by the knowledge that this part of the ridge is far less frequented than the rest, and that help may be some considerable distance and time away.]

[To reach the ridge from Coire a'Ghrunnda the most entertaining route is to the gap between Sgurr Dubh an Da Bheinn and Caisteal a'Garbh-choire. This approach involves easy scrambling on peridotite boulders that are extremely abrasive, and take their toll on fingers. More popular is the ascent to the Bealach a'Garbh-choire, which begins from near the southern end of the lochan, at a cairn. The route is not well defined, and a little scrambling is required.]

[This southern part of the ridge starts at Sgurr Dubh an Da Bheinn, and passes over a block of rock, the Caisteal a'Garbh-choire, Sgurr nan Eag and Sgurr a'Choire Bhig before the ridge ends at Gars-bheinn. Sgurr Dubh an Da Bheinn lies at the junction between the main ridge and the lateral ridge that leads eastwards to Sgurr Dubh Mor, a Munro. Sgurr nan Eag is the only other Munro. The linking ridge between Sgurr Dubh an Da Bheinn and Sgurr Dubh Mor involves moderate scrambling, with a few more awkward manoeuvres thrown in; this effectively rules out this inconveniently-placed Munro for walkers.]

[Caisteal a' Garbh-choire involves Very Difficult rock climbing, though this amazing block can be bypassed on either side, though some will find both possibilities intimidating.]

115

[Sgurr nan Eag is a huge mountain, with a long and level summit ridge. The highest point overlooks Coire nan Laogh. The ascent from Bealach a'Garbh-choire involves varied scrambling, quite hard in places if you stick to the crest. You can bypass any difficulties on the Coire a'Ghrunnda side, but these, too, involve scrambling.]

[The continuation to Sgurr a'Choire Bhig and Gars-bheinn also involves scrambling at variable standards, mixed with enjoyable but exposed walking across the typically rough terrain of the Cuillin. Gars-bheinn itself is flanked by interminable scree slopes on its south and west sides, and any walkers having succeeded in traversing the ridge from Coire a'Ghrunnda to Gars-bheinn will now be faced with a long and tiring descent by its south-west slope to the Allt Coire nan Laogh, followed by an even longer and even more tiring trek on the so-called 'coastal' path to Coruisk, across the moors back to Glen Brittle. Reversing this line to Gars-bheinn is punishing, gruelling and has little to commend it other than the views.]

WALK 3.17:
Loch an Fhir-Bhallaich

This fine mountain loch, unsuspected from below, lies at the base of Sgurr Dearg, and makes a perfect objective for a lazy summer evening, and as a leg-stretch for anyone confined all day to a tent by the vagaries of Skye weather.

Start/Finish: Glen Brittle memorial hut. GR.411216.
Distance: 6km (3¾ miles).
Ascent: 310m (1015 feet).

Begin along Walk 3.11 to Eas Mor, and, where the on-going path divides, branch right, up the moor towards the base of Sgurr Dearg. As Loch an Fhir-bhallaich is approached the path becomes boggy and crosses above the loch. Its setting is nothing spectacular, but this short tour is a worthwhile outing, and a splendid opportunity for walkers to get to know the Cuillin moors.

Pass on beyond the loch to reach the main path into Coire Lagan from the Glen Brittle campsite – indeed a diversion into Coire Lagan would not be out of place, though this extension would add about an hour to the walk overall.

Turn right to descend the Coire Lagan path until, just before reaching the fence behind the campsite toilet block, you can go right to the white cottage, An Dunan, from there crossing rough ground to a gate by Cuillin Cottage. An access track leads out to the road from the cottage, with just a short walk to the memorial hut remaining.

WALK 3.18:
Rubh' an Dùnain

Rubh' an Dùnain, the southernmost tip of the Minginish coast-line, is a place for incurable romantics, a 'grianan' – a sunny spot, or a secluded place for lovers. It is a place for peaceful wandering and exploration, a place of history, stronghold of the MacAskills, where once a small community flourished.

The walk to 'Roo' Point is easy and enjoyable, and only problem-atical when the descending burns of the southern Cuillin are in spate. Many visit Rubh' an Dùnain only when the Cuillin are hidden in mist, but this nostalgic spot deserves better, and merits a visit when the Cuillin heads are high in the blue sky and every detail starkly etched, for you will see this proud land for what it is, and feel the first caress of Skye's charming embrace.

Start/Finish: Glen Brittle campsite. GR.414204.
Distance: 11km (7 miles).
Ascent: Nominal; many ups and downs.

Cross the fence behind the campsite toilet block and turn right on a wet path below water storage tanks. There is a higher, broader, more distinct track above the tanks – you cross it when you take the path into Coire Lagan – and this makes progress considerably easier. For this reason, use it on the return journey.

The path meanders on, weaving around small boulders, and always with a good view across Loch Brittle to the islands of Rhum and Canna. In due course the path reaches the Allt Coire Lagan, and when the river is in spate it is not possible to cross it on the continuing line of the path, nor for that matter by the ford used by the higher track. Between the two, however, you will find a wooden footbridge. Once across, the simplest way of going on is to rise to the higher track and use that for its remaining short distance.

When the track ends, a clear path takes over and gradually approaches the cliffs of Creag Mhor. Just after a small burn, the path forks. One branch (left) climbs Creag Mhor, and gives a splendid view of the promontory ahead and the islands beyond. The lower path divides, with both alternatives rejoining a short way further. On the lower of these you cross the top of a fine, steep-sided ravine with the sea thrashing about below. Both the Creag Mhor route and the lower path eventually come to overlook a long wall crossing Slochd Dubh. Beyond the wall you can explore freely in the knowledge that simply by heading back towards the Cuillin you will at some point intersect this wall and can retrace your steps from there. This knowledge is especially important since the terrain is a vastly confusing series of lava waves that creates numerous bluffs and hollows, mini-cliffs and braes amid which walkers whose minds are in the Curiosity Department, seeking the traces of the past civilisations in which Rubh' an Dùnain abounds, may well become disorientated.

From the vicinity of Creag Mhor descend to cross the wall, rather towards the right. Beyond, the path traverses a boggy stretch of ground before finally reaching the top of a curious broad rock staircase leading down to fields where the traces of cultivation are quite distinct. Cross this open pasture to round a small brae, when you encounter another wall. Here, Loch na h-Airde comes into view, along with a chambered cairn and the remnants of a once-substantial house, Rhundunan, the ancestral home of the MacAskills.

More than one visit to Rubh' an Dùnain will be necessary before every corner is explored; on a first acquaintance be content with generally wandering about, and walking down to the point for a view across Soay Sound to the Isle of Soay, the Strathaird peninsula, and the steep slopes of Gars-bheinn, and out across the swelling seas to Rhum, Eigg and Canna. Or walk across to Sgeir Mhor, where seals often bask on the rocks.

On the return journey, you face directly at the Cuillin, with the recesses of Coire Lagan, Sgurr Dearg and the Inaccessible Pinnacle in view.

Rubh' an Dùnain
Rhundunan:

This was the home of the MacAskills, one of the oldest families in Skye, indeed there is a Gaelic tradition that "there was a MacAskall (sic) in Rudha as long as there was a MacLeod in Dunvegan". The last to hold Rubha was Hugh MacAskill, who died in 1864.

The MacAskills are traditionally said to be of Irish extraction, though the root, Asketill, meaning 'sacrificial vessel of the Gods', points to a Norse origin. It is said, too, that the MacAskills held Dun Sgathaich before the MacDonalds took possession, and, later, when reiving was at its height, that they acted as 'coastguards' for the MacLeods.

The land at Rubh' an Dùnain was cultivated for centuries, ending with the clearances of the nineteenth century.

Loch na h-Airde:

This idyllic loch is frequented by wildfowl and herons, and is only a few feet above sea level. Between loch and sea a man-made channel suggests that the nearby bay was a safe anchorage used, almost certainly, by the MacAskills, though the true origins of the channel are uncertain.

The Dun:

The position of this dun endorses the view that the MacAskills served as coast-watchers, though it would have served equally well to protect the cultivated land along the peninsula.

'Dun', although an ambiguous term, is a Scottish word describing a fortified dwelling place, usually a small coastal structure comprising a wall around a small sea cliff.

Chambered Cairn:

Chambered cairns are stone-built tombs, often megalithic in construction, and built by the early Neolithic farmers. The chambered cairn at Rubh' an Dùnain lies to the north of the loch, close by the wall. It is a remarkable structure with a central chamber in which artefacts of Neolithic and 'Beaker' pottery were found along with the bones of six adults. The site was excavated in 1932 by W Lindsay.

Cave:
Due east of the loch is a cave in a rock face that was used by Stone and Iron Age workers.

WALK 3.19:
Harta and Lota Corries

Most walkers exploring the Cuillin will sooner or later seek out Coruisk, for it is undoubtedly the one location that inspires everyone who sees it, set remote and rugged in the very heart of the mountains, quintessential Cuillin. Yet infinitely more accessible, especially from Sligachan, is a remote glen, much less attractive, it is true, but an excellent place for pedestrian exploration that will have no one clambering about on rocks in precarious positions. It is the U-shaped glen that rises first through Harta Corrie to the higher and smaller Lota Corrie, curving around Sgurr na h-Uamha, and flanked on the south and west by the long ridge of Druim nan Ramh. At the entrance to the corrie stands a shrub-encrusted boulder, the Bloody Stone, that features among the many tales of the clashes between the MacDonalds and the MacLeods. The approach to the Bloody Stone from Sligachan is a splendid walk, while the extension into the upper corrie, normally only used as a descent from the ridges above, nevertheless proves to be a fascinating place to explore.

> **Start/Finish:** Sligachan. GR.487299.
> **Distance:** 18km (11¼ miles)(maximum).
> **Height gain:** 250m (820 feet)(maximum).

The route into the corries takes the Coruisk path into Glen Sligachan until the point is reached where the River Sligachan turns sharply into the corrie: two cairns on the Sligachan path mark the spot where you leave it for the Harta Corrie path, cutting down to the river, and keeping to its true right bank.

Not far from the entrance to the corrie stands the Bloody Stone, a strange and isolated boulder more than 10m (30 feet) high. Beyond the Bloody Stone the path gradually disappears as the corrie narrows and curves around the base of Sgurr na h-Uamha. Here it is that the hitherto level going acquires a gradient, rising shortly to the upper reaches of Harta Corrie directly beneath the massive crags of An Caisteal.

A water chute, a satisfactory terminus for this walk, flows down the head of the corrie, and is a spectacular site following rain. Lota Corrie lies above the chute, and the route to it cairned.

The Bloody Stone

In 1395 the MacDonalds sent a powerful force in galleys to invade Skye. Evading the vigilance of the MacAskills at Rubh' an Dùnain, the hereditary coast-watchers of the MacLeods, the invaders landed at Loch Eynort and rapidly progressed east towards Sligachan leaving a trail of devastation behind them. At Sligachan, however, they met a formidable force of MacLeods, and a furious battle ensued during which the invaders were thrown into confusion which soon became a rout. The MacLeods ruthlessly pursued them back to Loch Eynort where, with cruel fate, the MacAskills had seized their galleys and moored them off-shore. It is said that not one of the invaders survived, and that the heads of the slain were collected, numbered and sent to Dunvegan as trophies to be retained in the custody of the warden of Dunvegan Castle. It was at Creag an Fheannaidh, The Rock of the Flaying, now known as the Bloody Stone, that the spoils of battle were divided.

Quite how watertight this tale might be is open to question for it is known that the leader of the invading army, Alasdair Carrach, was living in 1398 — he is mentioned in a document of that date — and that he must have been living in 1431, when his lands were forfeited for insurrection. The substance of the tale, however, remains unchallenged, and lends a certain macabre aspect to this walk into the dark depths of Harta Corrie.

WALK 3.20:
Druim Hain and Sgurr Na Stri

Said to be named following a boundary dispute between the MacLeods and the MacKinnons, Sgurr na Stri (the Peak of Strife), although a minor peak by Cuillin standards, holds such a commanding position at the head of Loch Scavaig that its ascent is eminently justified. Its two highest summits are dramatic vantage points respectively for the sanctum of Coruisk and the bay of Camasunary.

Scramblers may find a selection of routes to this summit from around the coastline, but for walkers there remains just one route, a most excellent excursion from Sligachan, that serves well anyone making a first visit to the Cuillin, giving an idea of the sort of terrain and time to be expected in future exploits.

The top of Sgurr na Stri is a very complex arrangement of rocky outcrops, and its ascent must not be contemplated in less than perfect weather conditions. By the same token, the overall distance of this walk should not be underestimated. After prolonged rain the path through Glen Sligachan is often awash and in places impassable without a long and tiring detour. Keep in mind that everything you encounter on the outward route needs to be tackled again on the return journey, unless you plan to continue with the glen route to Camasunary.

Start/Finish: Sligachan. GR.487299.
Distance: 23km (14¼ miles).
Ascent: 565m (1855 feet).

From Sligachan take the footpath heading into the glen, signposted to Loch Coruisk. The path, dominated in its early stages by the tower of Sgurr nan Gillean, heads relentlessly into the glen, encountering numerous feeder burns before reaching the rather more substantial Allt na Measarroch. Cross the burn, almost always a wet proposition, and continue to a prominent boulder, Clach na Craoibhe Chaoruinn.

More pleasant walking beneath the great slopes of Marsco brings you to a branching of ways, not far past the two Lochan Dubha, and at the entrance to Am Fraoch-choire. Here take the right branch, and shortly start the climb to a large cairn on Druim Hain, from where both Loch Scavaig and Loch Coruisk come into view for the first time.

The onward route is now a little confusing and requires concentration. Immediately below lies Coire Riabhach, and the main path seems to head for this, but only leads to a viewpoint, though this is well worth the diversion. The correct path goes left (south) to another cairn, where it forks once more. The right branch leads down to Coruisk, taking a slanting line down through Coire Riabach to reach the loch below, and should therefore be ignored.

For Sgurr na Stri, take the left branch at this point as it continues more or less level across the hillside below Sgurr Hain to reach a prominent monument, Captain Maryon's Cairn, a stone pyramid erected by friends of the captain, whose body was found here in 1948, two years after he disappeared.

About 5 minutes (and no more) after leaving the monument, look for a stream draining a grassy hollow on the left, and ascend through this to reach the top of Sgurr na Stri. Return by the same route. Do not attempt any descent of the flanks of Sgurr na Stri.

WALK 3.21:
Loch Coruisk

None of the early visitors to Skye had anything good to say about Loch Coruisk and its surrounds. Dr John MacCulloch, who toured the Highlands from 1811 to 1821, claimed of Coruisk that "Here the sun never shone since creation", a fanciful, and inexact, observation. Walter Scott, who sailed to the Hebrides in 1814, landed at Loch Scavaig and walked up to Coruisk, later recounting his experience in The Lord of the Isles, *and denying Coruisk anything but "rocks at random thrown, black waves, bare crags, and banks of stone". Even in his diary he was little more enthusiastic: "Vegetation there was little or none, and the mountains rose...perpendicularly from the water's edge".*

Inevitably, The Lord of the Isles *was instrumental in firing the curiosity of those with the means to venture into such remote places, with Coruisk always high on their respective lists of places to visit. When H V Morton came* In Search of Scotland, *he found Coruisk "the grandest and most gloomy view in the British Isles. Mountains all round me, the sinister Coolins forming a gigantic barrier to the west, and below, like some deep, dark jewel, the rock-bound waters of the loch, pale green at the edges and green-black in the depths, fretted by wind into a million ripples".*

Legend has it that a cave by the loch is inhabited by the ghost of a shepherd who spends his time perpetually branding the ghost of a sheep, the latter's cries being clearly heard above the wind.

The beauty of Coruisk, in spite of the early misrepresentations of it, lies in the complete absence of restraint; here the powers of creation have fashioned a scene of wild and rugged grandeur. The loch bears a number of small islands, and is ringed by sandy bays. All around lie boulders, rocks and heather, while the towering ramparts of the Cuillin spill streams into suspended corries, over crags, and down to the loch. Shapes bizarre and colours rich blend in profusion, over-burdening the senses, alarming the timid, inspiring the heroic, and, in essence, providing arguably the most outstanding location on Skye that walkers may wish to find.

There are a few ways into Coruisk across the line of the main ridge, but none of these is available to walkers, and should only be contemplated by the most experienced of Skye mountaineers. Likewise the so-called coastal path from Glen Brittle, which involves some very complex route-finding and awkward passages in precarious positions; this, too, must be avoided.

Slightly easier, but no less daunting, and for that reason also to be avoided, is the approach from Camasunary. This begins by fording a tidal river, difficult at the best of times and impossible when the tide is in, or after prolonged rain. There used to be a precarious bridge here, but that disappeared in the mid-1980s. The route then pursues a sketchy and water-logged trail around the base of Sgurr na Stri, until, within site of the entrance to Coruisk, you encounter the Bad Step. This takes the form of a huge and steep slab of convex rock that drops directly into the waters of Loch na Leachd. A crack slants upwards across the face of the rock, but its ascent (or descent) *requires scrambling skills and a good nerve, since a slip will end in deep water. Without scrambling skills, Loch Coruisk cannot be reached by this route.*

Thankfully, walkers are not denied access to Coruisk, though the approach and retreat is long and arduous. It should not be contemplated in poor visibility, or fickle weather conditions.

Start/Finish: Sligachan. GR.487299.
Distance: 22km (13¾ miles)(minimum).
Ascent: 515m (1690 feet).

Follow Walk 3.20 as far as the large cairn on Druim Hain, and take the left of two on-going paths (south) to another cairn, where the path forks again. The Coruisk path here branches right, and slants down through Coire Riabhach to reach the loch.

Once in the Coruisk sanctum the extent of your exploration will be determined by the recent state of the weather. Theoretically you can walk all around the loch. There is a boggy path all the way, and stepping stones not far from Loch Scavaig, but success in this endeavour is determined by the amount of water flowing into the corrie, and the numerous burns that are frequently found in spate or near spate conditions, when they become impassable. Any exploration has to be tempered with the knowledge of what will be involved in making a retreat. And keep in mind that the waters of the loch have been known to rise 2.5m (8 feet+) in a day.

Having explored, return over Druim Hain by your outward route.

WALK 3.22:
Glen Brittle Forest walk
(An Cruachan: Beinn Staic)

Unlike most forest walks, this circular tour of the Glen Brittle Forest seldom feels enclosed, and provides good views, especially of Loch Eynort and the Cuillin summits above Coire a'Ghreadaidh and Coire na Creiche. An ideal excursion for a 'rest' day, and on which to study the range of trees in the forest — sitka spruce, Corsican pine, Japanese larch, Austrian pine, goat willow, alder and Douglas fir.

Start/Finish: Forest picnic site. GR.423263.
Distance: 15km (9½ miles).
Ascent: 255m (835 feet).

From the picnic area walk uphill along the road to reach a gate on the left just before the forest boundary. Go through the gate and follow a broad forest trail, ignoring a left fork soon after entering the forest. Stay on the twisting main trail for over 3km (2 miles), with improving glimpses of Glen Eynort and later Loch Eynort. Forest clearance has done much to enhance the views, which maintain interest throughout the walk.

On reaching a junction, where a path descends, right, into Glen Eynort, keep left, and climb to another junction at a wide U-bend at the head of a ravine. Go right, and follow a balcony trail high above Loch Eynort, with ever-increasing views seawards, until you reach a T-junction. Turn left, and soon cross the infant Allt Dabhoch, hidden in a mature spread of trees, and soon, at another junction keep ahead, ignoring the right branch to Kraiknish.

Now the route climbs energetically to the bare Bealach Brittle, bursting from the trees below the craggy dome of Beinn Staic. As you advance, so the spread of the central Cuillins opens up before you, the path swinging round, left, to re-enter forest. When the main trail divides, go right, and keep going until you reach the Glen Brittle road, and there turn left to begin a steady uphill plod back to the picnic site.

Variations:
Walkers seeking out only the two minor summits, An Cruachan and Beinn Staic will find it easiest to reach Bealach Brittle by reversing the above route, entering the forest, just above the roadbridge, at GR.419249.

3.22a: An Cruachan
From Bealach Brittle it is possible to go south-west, through a gate, and over trackless moorland to engage An Cruachan's outstanding

Crossing Bealach Brittle

view of the Cuillins, especially around Coire Lagan, Loch Eynort and the southern Outer Hebrides. Some of the going is rough (though the overall walking is fairly easy), and a final steepening pull is needed to reach the trig pillar and rocky summit.

Very rough going links An Cruachan and Truagh Mheall, with no tracks to aid progress; the 'easiest' approach is from the south-west, the effort, for such minor tops, only compensated by the fine view of Loch Brittle, and the long, low thumb of Rubh' an Dùnain.

3.22b: Beinn Staic
From Bealach Brittle climb steeply, north-east, by the edge of the forest and use a short stretch of zigzag track before finishing up steep grass to the summit plateau.

WALK 3.23:
Talisker Bay and Fiskavaig

Although brief, this walk is not an easy day option, being largely over rough and trackless terrain that is invariably and excessively wet. You need good navigational skills for this route, and a genuine liking for plotting detours across a complex landscape. Much reward lies, however, in the opportunity to investigate the Talisker Bay sea cliffs, to visit the superb viewpoint of Rubha Cruinn, and to wander northwards to Loch Bracadale, returning by an ancient broch and cross-country trail. Talisker lies at the foot of Gleann Oraid, worthy of road-bound pedestrian survey in itself. The Bay is dominated by the massive prow of Preashal More, and its sandy beach enjoys much popularity on every fair day during the tourist season.

Samuel Johnson and James Boswell visited Talisker, regarded by the latter as "a better place than one commonly finds in Sky (sic)", on 23 September 1773. "Before it is a wide expanse of sea, on each hand of which are immense rocks; and, at some distance in the sea, there are three columnal rocks rising to sharp points. The billows break with prodigious force and noise on the coast of Talisker". Johnson, however, who did not care for the wilder places of Britain, was less complimentary, saying: "Talisker is the place beyond all that I have seen from which the gay and the jovial seem utterly excluded, and where the hermit might expect to grow old in meditation, without the possibility of disturbance or interruption".

Talisker has its place in Skye legend as the spot where Cuchullin, the Hero of Ulster, having taken two strides from the northern tip of Ireland, landed on Skye, bound for Skiach's school for heroes in the mountains, from where she taught the art of war.

Across the bay the sea cliffs stand impressively dark, gashed vertically by a great waterfall, and this is your first objective.

Start/Finish: Talisker, at the end of public road. GR.326306. The approach by road is from Carbost on Loch Harport. Park tidily at the end of the public road, taking especial care not to cause obstruction.
Distance: 9½km (6 miles).
Ascent: 170m (557 feet).

From the parking space turn right, down a track, to pass Talisker Farm, shortly crossing the River Talisker by a footbridge. As you approach A'Chailleach, go left through an iron gate to gain an old track that zigzags up the hillside ahead. Follow this only to the first

Talisker Bay
Preashal Mhor

On Oronsay
The Coral Beach

hairpin bend, and there leave it and cross a small stream. Now climb the grassy, outcropped hillside beyond to reach the top of the cliff edge. Take care not to stray too far inland unless intent on visiting the soggy sanctuary of Loch an Sgùirr Mhóir. Once the cliffs of Sròn Mhór have been reached, virtually all the uphill work is done, and all that remains is to soak in (sometimes literally) the wilderness of this stretch of the Minginish coastline.

Before long, making what use you can of sheep traces above Sròn Mhór, you reach the Allt Mheididh, the stream that plummets over the cliff edge to the crashing waves below. It is not uncommon for spray from the waterfall to be blown back upwards by the wind, arcing high to drench unsuspecting passers-by. Ahead, the view of Rubha Cruinn is quite breathtaking, while to the south, the vertical cliffs of Biod Ruadh stand starkly etched against the sky.

Rubha Cruinn is an outstanding vantage point, and, if you can find shelter from the prevailing wind, a perfect place for a halt. Indeed, this isolated outpost makes a fine objective in itself, and a direct retracing of your outward steps does nothing to lessen the pleasure of the walk.

The continuation northwards requires serious thought. You move further away from help with every stride, and the conditions, rough and uncompromising, never relax. Good map-reading is vital here.

From Rubha Cruinn, cross the moor to the top of Sgùrr Mor, resisting any temptation to look for an easier way along the inviting grass shelf down below, near McFarlane's Rock. As you reach Sgùrr Mor, so you get your first glimpse of MacLeod's Maidens on Idrigill Point to the north-west. A network of sheep tracks provides some relief and eases progress across a marvellous landscape of rock formations, ravines, steep-sided inlets, and sweeping moorland. On your trek northwards look out for an immense rock bowl down on the shore, a huge cauldron, carved by the sea.

Further on a detour is needed to evade the clutches of a deep-cut ravine that carves into the tussocky moorland plateau. Beyond this it becomes impossible to give meaningful directions; the terrain is chaotic, the rock outcrops confusing, but your objective is the obvious high ground ahead, of Rubha nan Clach, where you will be rewarded with a fine view of Loch Bracadale.

Beyond Ruadh nan Clach, onward progress is again hampered

by complex terrain, lashed by burns and ravines, many steep-sided and dangerous. The easiest option is to keep as high as you can above the burns, before they become too deep-sided, and to head for Dùn Ard an t-Sabhail, a broch, the remains of which lie in splendid isolation on the rocky summit of a conspicuous hill, about 1½km (1 mile) due east of Ruadh nan Clach.

On leaving the broch, head south-east, and after about 10-15 minutes of squelchy progress you will intersect a cross-country trail running south from the hairpin bend in the road south of Fiskavaig. For a while there is some respite from waterlogged progress, but as you cross a tributary of Huisgill Burn, boggy ground returns. But now the end is in sight, albeit not yet literally. This cross-moor track leads unerringly back to A'Chailleach, and the zigzag path leading down to Talisker Bay, from where you can retrace your steps.

WALK 3.24:
Oronsay from Ullinish

The island of Oronsay is but one of a number dotted about Loch Bracadale; its distinction being that you can walk on to it at low tide. When the tides co-operate, a trip to the island in the evening to watch the sun go down is a memorable experience, but be sure to carry a torch as it goes dark quickly on Skye.

Oronsay is a tilted, wedge-shaped island, rising in a carpet of luxurious green from the waters of Loch Bracadale, to vertical cliffs more than 70m (235 feet) in height. An hour or two resting on this splendid perch, watching fishing boats, seals, the occasional basking shark, twite, skylarks, gannets, fulmars and gulls, will be remembered as a time of simple contentment.

Start/Finish: Road junction/bend, near Ullinish Lodge Hotel, reached from the A863. GR.324377.
Distance: 4km (2¼miles).
Ascent: 100m (330 feet).

From the sharp bend near the Ullinish Lodge, go through a gate near an isolated building and turn acutely left round the building to find a grassy path, not immediately obvious (head towards a fence), that leads to a small gate giving access to a narrow tarmac lane. The same point may be reached by walking down the lane from the road to the Ullinish Lodge.

On reaching the road, go right, until the road ends near a house. Pass through a gate, and take to a rough track across open meadow, with improving views west and north-west to MacLeod's Tables and the islands of Loch Bracadale. The track deteriorates to a path, but is never in doubt, and leads you to the causeway at Ullinish Point. Go through a gate, and descend a rocky gully to the bouldery beach.

It is important that you cross to Oronsay AS THE TIDE IS GOING OUT, if you want to avoid an unscheduled stay on this uninhabited, waterless island.

There are a few paths on the island, but none is needed. Simply explore freely, taking in the light at Ardtreck, the great sea cliffs below Fiskavaig, and the far, hazy Cuillins, as you work your way to the highest point. The cliffs come as a surprise, and there is no barrier against a spectacular fall in the event of a slip. So do take care! When you have dined sufficiently on this banquet of peace and solitude, simply retrace your steps.

The low tide causeway to Oronsay

131

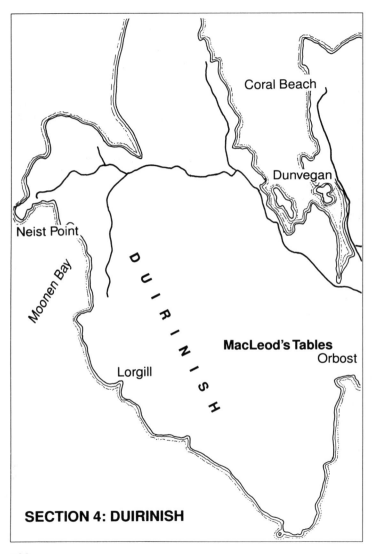

Coral Beach

Dunvegan

Neist Point

Moonen Bay

D U I R I N I S H

MacLeod's Tables
Orbost

Lorgill

SECTION 4: DUIRINISH

SECTION 4:
Duirinish

The Duirinish peninsula provides some of the most spectacular and breathtaking walking outwith the Cuillin, and lies west of Loch Dunvegan and Loch Bracadale, though the full extent of Duirinish might be said to include the short wedge of land projecting northwards from Dunvegan to Loch Bay.

Access to the region is by the B884, south of Dunvegan, from which one road runs briefly to Orbost, while the main road continues to the widely-spread crofting community of Glen Dale at the southern edge of Loch Pooltiel. From Glen Dale another road runs to the isolated farmstead at Ramasaig, while a shorter road runs out to Waterstein and Neist Point, the most westerly point on Skye.

There are few hills in Duirinish, the notable exception being MacLeod's Tables, but the coastal walking must rank alongside the finest in Britain. Almost 30km (20 miles) of virtually uninhabited coastline between Orbost and Waterstein can be consumed by the superfit in one mighty endeavour, but needs transport at both ends, while shorter circuits may be made that will allow everyone to savour this delectable corner of Skye.

The most popular excursion is to the impressive sea stacks off Idrigill Point, the MacLeod's Maidens. Beyond Idrigill Point the coastline becomes increasingly dramatic with a fascinating natural architecture of cliffs, stacks, caves and geos (steep-sided inlets from the sea). The walking generally keeps close to cliff tops, following sheep tracks across close-cropped turf.

This is an area walkers can have to themselves, for there is little here to interest rock climbers and scramblers, but the coastline is remote from outside help, and walks should not be undertaken in poor weather conditions.

WALK 4.1:
Loch Bharcasaig, Idrigill Point and MacLeod's Maidens

The finest sea stacks on Skye lie off Idrigill Point; they are the MacLeod's Maidens. The highest of these is the tallest on Skye, and rises to almost 65m (210 feet). This walk, to the viewpoint on the nearby cliff, is one of the most outstanding coastal walks on the Island. For most of the way it follows a fairly well-contoured path, though new forestry work around Brandersaig Bay will need time to settle and become established. Imaginatively, Forest Enterprise has created a fine variety of green foliage and a number of exciting vistas through the forest, replacing many conifers with new broad-leaved trees, notably alongside the burns and at the forest boundaries. On-going forestry work may change the route description slightly over the years.

To reach the start of the walk at Orbost, leave the A863 either at Heribost and go down through Roag to Orbost, or at Lonmore (B884), then by a minor road to Orbost. The metalled road surface ends at Orbost House, and though it is possible to drive a rough track a short distance further, it is rather bumpy. It may be better to try to find a parking place along the main peninsula road, or go behind Orbost House to park on a flat area of turf, taking care not to cause obstruction.

Start/Finish: Orbost. GR.256434.
Distance: 16km (10 miles).
Ascent: 350m (1150 feet).

Go past Orbost Farm and Orbost House, and down a rough farm access track to reach Loch Bharcasaig, a delightful starting point, its dark, pebbly beach framed on the right by the wooded slopes of Cnoc na Pairce and on the left by the low headland of Meall Greepa.

Across the bay, tackle the Abhainn Bharcasaig by a sturdy wooden bridge giving on to a broad track into the older part of the forest. The path through this section ambles along pleasantly, with occasional views across the bay, and glimpses of Beinn na Boineid inland.

Shortly after leaving the forest you cross Forse Burn to climb a steep slope on a rocky path (cairned). Before long you meet new plantings which obscure some parts of the original path. Generally, keep ahead. The on-going path is cairned and leads to a steady rise to the bealach between Beinn na Boineid and Beinn na Moine, which is marked by a cairn.

Keep descending from the bealach across the hillsides above Brandarsaig Bay. When you meet a fence follow it round to rejoin the original path, which continues down to the deserted crofts of Brandarsaig. Cross Brandarsaig Burn and go left up a brae beyond which the path crosses the moor and goes down to a fence near Idrigill Burn. Beyond the burn, climb to a wide area of grassland and the ruins of Idrigill, where, running down to the turf dyke at the cliff edge, there are some of the finest and best known examples on Skye of the lazybed method of cultivation.

The walk now heads inland on a good path through Glac Ghealaridh, a pleasant heather carpet between low hills. Once beyond the two small hills – Steineval and Ard Beag – the path is less prominent and passes more ruins as it steers south-west towards Idrigill Point. Here the path rounds the bay, Inbhir a'Ghàrraidh. Abandon the path and head for the cliff top, with care, following it south for a fine view of the Maidens. The whole of this final section is a confusing terrain of hummocks and hollows that make it impossible to keep to a direct line. There is a cairn on the cliff top directly above the Maidens, but the cliff edge is a precarious and crumbling place, and requires utmost care.

Return, leisurely, by your outward route.

MacLeod's Maidens

Legend relates that the three stacks were so named when the wife and two daughters of the Fourth Chief of the Clan MacLeod perished there in a boat that had drifted before a strong westerly wind across the Minch from Harris, to be pounded to pieces on the Maidens.

The largest of the Maidens is said to be not unlike statues of a seated Queen Victoria when seen from the sea. She is the

Mother, and is said to be constantly weaving. Walter Scott called the Maidens the 'Choosers of the Slain' in an allusion to the last appearance of the Valkyries over this part of Skye as they fled before the coming Christianity. It was the custom of the Valkyries to weave a web of death before a battle, and then choose the best and bravest of the slain and lead them to Valhalla.

The Maidens, too, are notorious wreckers of ships, some say aided by the practice of smuggler Campbell of Ensor, who used the Black Skerries at the Maidens' feet to position false lights.

WALK 4.2:
Glen Ollisdal and MacLeod's Maidens

This alternative way of reaching MacLeod's Maidens is far more demanding, has fewer continuous paths (in some places none at all), and should not be attempted without good navigational skills and settled weather.

   Start/Finish: Orbost. GR.256434.
   Distance: 19km (12 miles).
   Ascent: 400m (1310 feet).

Begin as for Walk 4.1 to reach the shores of Loch Bharcasaig, and climb the steep bank along the boundary of Bharcasaig Forest, keeping to the path that follows the northern edge of the forest. For a while this is tightly pressed between the forest and the slopes of An Cruachan, but is followed until the fence starts to descend to the Abhainn Bharcasaig. Now leave the fence and make a gradual ascent along the north side of a tributary burn to reach the Bealach Bharcasaig, across which there are the low remains of a turf dyke.

Follow the course of the turf dyke until it disappears in an area of bogs. Traverse these bogs and climb the slope beyond until you see and can then pass the Ollisdal Lochs, keeping them on your right, by using the slopes of Beinn Bhac-ghlais. Once beyond the bogs, gradually trend right and cross the River Ollisdal above Coire Mor. Descend steeply into the corrie, heading for a building (Ollisdal bothy) that soon appears. As you descend so it becomes easier to traverse grassy slopes on the right to approach the bothy.

Beyond the bothy, cross the burn and stay along its left bank to the cliffs of Ollisdal Geo, a steep-sided inlet. Turn south-east and climb easily to the top of Biod a'Mhurain, which proves to be a superb lookout. A gentle descent then leads to one of the most stunning viewpoints around the coast of Skye where the Lorgasdal River plummets to the sea. Rocky reefs, a natural arch (one of many around the Duirinish coastline), and crumbling sea stacks make a splendid sight.

The Lorgasdal River must be forded, and to do this a short detour is needed inland, beyond which you make a steady ascent across the base of Ben Idrigill. Gradually the MacLeod's Maidens loom larger with the best view being from the cliffs of Inbhir a'Ghàrraidh.

Three burns feed into Inbhir a'Ghàrraidh, and all these need slight detours, following sheep tracks that have been well trodden by walkers. The on-going path does not approach the viewpoint directly above MacLeod's Maidens, and to see them you will need to abandon it for a while.

The rest of the walk reverses Walk 4.1, and is largely well defined and cairned. It begins by heading for, Glac Ghealaridh, a heather-rich glen between Steineval and Ard Beag.

As you leave the valley keep north on a path away from the cliffs, and then resume the well-trodden route back to Orbost. New forestry work might pose a few brief problems until a pathway is re-established through it, but the correct line is usually easy to detect, and climbs to the bealach between Beinn na Boineid and Beinn na Moine.

The main forest is entered beyond Forse Burn, and provides a good track back to Loch Bharcasaig. The ruins of Idrigill and Brandarsaig crofting settlements will inject even further interest during the final stages of this rewarding walk.

WALK 4.3:
Lorgill Bay

This short and easy walk visits the site of one of Skye's long lost communities, at Lorgill, and is another poignant reminder of the troubled times of the Clearances. The ruins of many of the former cottages can still be found on either side of the Lorgill River. For all its charm, life in Lorgill must have been harsh and isolated, even at the end of the twentieth century hallmarked by a remoteness that is hard to believe.

Start/Finish: Ramasaig Farm. GR.165441. Park tidily, off-road, near the large sheep enclosure.
Distance: 6½km (4 miles).
Ascent: 140m (460 feet).

Cross the nearby bridge, and go through the small gate beyond, then passing to the right of farm buildings. As you round the buildings so you join a broad track that leads you unerringly across the moor towards the defile of the Lorgill River beyond. On the way you pass the remains of an old shieling beside the track that is worth a moment's inspection.

Within half an hour the track begins to descend, through another gate, to the northern end of the wide ravine of Lorgill. Leave the track beyond the gate at its first bend, and follow a grassy path through numerous remains of cottages. Here the rich green pastures are a delight, and may be traversed all the way to the beach, the first break in the long line of the Duirinish cliffs since Loch Bhacarsaig, beyond Idrigill Point.

Lorgill

Like many crofting communities on Skye, Lorgill suffered during the Clearances. Ten families lived at Lorgill, and in 1830 they were read the following statement by the sheriff officer:

> *"To all the crofters in Lorgill. Take notice that you are hereby duly warned that you all be ready to leave Lorgill at twelve*

o'clock on the 4th August next with all your baggage but no stock and proceed to Loch Snizort, where you will board the ship Midlothian (Captain Morrison) that will take you to Nova-Scotia, where you are to receive a free grant of land from Her Majesty's Government. Take further notice that any crofter disobeying this order will be immediately arrested and taken to prison. All persons over seventy years of age and who have no relatives to look after them will be taken care of in the County Poorhouse. This order is final and no appeal to the Government will be considered. God Save the Queen."

Lorgill, of course, was not the only village left empty in this way, and families were evicted from other parts of Duirinish, Bracadale and Minginish. Between 1841 and 1881, the population that existed in 1824 was halved, with tenant farmers replacing the crofters.

WALK 4.4:
The Hoe and Ramasaig Bay

This circuit of the high cliffs of Duirinish between Lorgill and Ramasaig Bay provides magnificent views and relaxed walking on pleasant turf. In a few places, the path — largely constructed from linking sheep tracks — passes close to the edge of the cliffs and requires care at all times, and a wide berth in windy conditions.

Please note that dogs are not allowed on The Hoe, where there is too great a risk of startling sheep.

Start/Finish: Ramasaig Farm. GR.165441. Park tidily, off-road, near the large sheep enclosure.
Distance: 8km (5 miles).
Ascent: 300m (985 feet).

From Ramasaig take the track across the moor to Lorgill as described in Walk 4.3. As you pass through the gate above Lorgill and start descending the broad track, leave the main track, near a ruined cottage, at the first bend, and cut diagonally downwards, passing by a number of ruined buildings.

Along the cliffs of Duirinish

The atmosphere is one of calm and peace, and the greensward a delight to walk on. As you head towards the beach, cradled by dark cliffs, so you encounter a fence. Cross this at a spot where there is nominal protection from its barbs, and then continue through more ruins to reach the rocky shore.

When you are ready to leave the beach, your objective is to climb the hillside to the west. Locate the remains of a crumbling and overgrown intake wall, and climb, steeply for a while, using linking sheep tracks, trending diagonally left. Do not keep to the lower tracks since these only lead to steep and dangerous grassy slopes.

Once beyond the initial steepness, the remaining walking is pure delight, and should be savoured at a relaxed pace. The seaward views are outstanding, while the cliffs are frequented by a range of sea birds, notably cormorants, shags, oystercatchers, herring gulls and fulmars; seals often appear just off-shore. Gradually the grassy slopes rise to meet a fence, which leads you on across the lower shoulder of the highest point, The Hoe, to which a short diversion is needed, though there is little but uninteresting moorland beyond, the views of MacLeod's Tables and the Cuillin being too distant to hold much appeal.

From the high point, the subsequent descent to Hoe Rape (follow it right to the end) is superb. Most of the seabirds nesting on the cliffs are fulmars, and during the breeding season do not take kindly to visitors, and become aggressive in their behaviour — be prepared to duck! Better still, avoid the walk altogether in the breeding season.

From the delightful little headland of Hoe Rape, turn inland, but still following the coastline. Gradually you come down to the rocky beach of Ramasaig Bay, bright in spring with thrift and rose-root, and a mesmeric spot.

Soon you cross the Abhainn an Lòin Bhàin above the shore. Go through a gate, following an old green track before it peters out, leaving you to pursue tractor trails through the Ramasaig fields back to the farm buildings at the start of the walk.

WALK 4.5:
Duirinish Coastal Path

There are few who would contest that the walk from Loch Bharcasaig, past Idrigill Point and MacLeod's Maidens, to the deserted village of Lorgill, ranks as the finest cliff top walk in Britain. The scenery is breathtaking throughout the walk, and seems never-ending as each new headland presents ever more delights.

This is an essential route for any walker visiting Skye, though it presents a few logistical problems. Not the least of these is that it is 22km (almost 14 miles) between the two road ends, at Orbost and Ramasaig, and requires two cars. By ending the walk at Lorgill, you could trek across country back to your starting point, via the Bealach Bharcasaig, but this will add 8km (5 miles) to the walk, and requires good navigational skills and plenty of energy.

Other possibilities include pre-pitching a tent at Lorgill, camping overnight, and then walking back the next day — not as preposterous a suggestion as might be supposed, since the walk is just as thrilling in a north-south direction. If you can arrange transport to both ends, then the possibility arises of extending the walk (nominally) by finishing over The Hoe to Ramasaig Bay, rather than cutting inland at Lorgill.

You are asked not to take dogs on this walk, even on a lead. The route passes perilously close to high cliffs at times, and invites the quite unacceptable risk of startling sheep that graze on the luxurious turf along the top of the cliffs.

Although a path is shown on the maps, in reality it does not exist. Progress, however, is effected by way of an almost continual line of sheep tracks. The terrain is excellent throughout the walk, and poses few problems. Postpone the walk on very windy days.

> **Start:** Orbost. GR.256434.
> **Finish:** Ramasaig. GR.165441.
> **Distance:** 22km (13¾ miles).
> **Ascent:** 530m (1740 feet).

The walk begins by following Walk 4.1 as far as Idrigill Point and MacLeod's Maidens. From there follow the cliff top around Inbhir a'Ghàrraidh and across the slopes of Ben Idrigill as they flow down to the cliffs. Descend slightly to cross a burn and on to the next headland, from where the route stretches ahead to distant Lorgill Bay and The Hoe.

The next section of coastline, across Glen Lorgasdal and onwards, is quite outstanding. The cliffs are decorated with numerous stacks and pinnacles, and one has a fine natural arch, best seen looking back once the Lorgasdal River is crossed.

Press on around the next headland to reach Glen Ollisdal, and on to Glen Dibidal. Glen Dibidal (the Deep Glen) is a steep-sided ravine, and requires a slanting diversion inland to cross it safely, above the ravine.

Resuming the cliff top route the coastline becomes more dramatic, well adorned with caves and arches, though care is needed if you are to see them to good advantage since many stretches of the cliffs here are overhanging and fragile. The first of these appears as you cross the burn draining from Loch an Fhridhein, and soon you encounter a fence along the top of the cliff, with more arches beyond.

Gradually you climb around a small cove from the top of which you can catch your last glimpse of MacLeod's Maidens (unless you continue across The Hoe). Keep along the cliff edge, and descend gradually to cross Scaladal Burn, when another massive cave appears ahead. As you reach Scaladal Burn you must follow the ravine inland to find a sheep track descending into it above a waterfall, climbing out of it on a stepped rock ledge. Next comes another pull up to Biod Boidheach, the Beautiful Cliff, its luxurious green sward and steep-edged profile very appropriately named, before a long and gentle descent alongside a fence to Lorgill.

If continuing across The Hoe (Walk 4.4) you can often cross the Lorgill River near the beach, where it broadens out. But otherwise, or if it is in spate, you need to trek inland to cross the river safely near a renovated barn.

Once across the river, follow an ascending track to an intake gate, and then by a broad cart track across the moor to Ramasaig.

WALK 4.6:
Waterstein Head

Perched high above the waters of Moonen Bay, once fished by Gavin Maxwell for basking shark from his base on the Isle of Soay, Waterstein Head is one of the most spectacular cliffs on the Island, a magnificent eyrie from which to gaze out across the Minch to the Outer Hebrides floating on the far horizon.

Start/Finish: Small parking area at the summit of the road above Loch Mòr. GR.148488.
Distance: 4km (2½ miles).
Ascent: 185m (605 feet).

The way out to Waterstein Head is quite simple to follow, making use of a prominent escarpment directly above Loch Mòr.

From the parking area head for a turf dyke, and follow this up the escarpment. Shortly after tackling a fence, you cross a small ravine. Then, as the escarpment becomes a steep slope, Waterstein Head finally appears, reached by following a fence that shepherds you up the final section to the summit.

Across the sea the Outer Hebrides present an interesting challenge of identification, while much closer the finger of Neist Point probes into the wave-fringed expanse of Moonen Bay. But it is the stunning view of the restless sea that commands greatest attention, and makes the modest effort of ascent well worthwhile.

WALK 4.7:
Neist Point Lighthouse

This mini outing to Neist Point, the most westerly point on Skye, needs no detailed description, since following a prescribed route is less important than exploration. In any event, a concrete path leads from the parking space above the Point, all the way to the lighthouse.

Neist Point and Moonen Bay which it embraces is dominated by the prow of Waterstein Head (Walk 4.6), and a satisfactory day can be spent visiting both – tackle Waterstein Head first, and then descend by road to Neist Point.

The two short walks are very different in character, the one dramatic and inspiring at the top of one of Skye's most impressive sea cliffs, the other filled with places of interest and a wildlife spectacular that is amazing. Neist is a magnetic place, to which you will be drawn many times, and has a nasty habit of consuming more time than might be supposed from a cursory glance at the map.

From the parking space the lighthouse path lies beyond a gate adjoining storage sheds, and winds down and across an escarpment face well endowed with wild flowers, ferns and heather. The path reaches a wide grassy plateau, which you can cross to reach a minor sea cliff (keep children under control here) from which to inspect the higher cliffs of An t-Aigeach beyond, on which, strange as it may seem given the popularity of the Cuillin, rock gymnasts have fashioned some of the hardest routes on Skye.

Neist Point

Young basking sharks often frequent these coastal waters, which they share with seals and, at a distance, killer whales. But it is the birdlife that will astound, and bird-watchers should go well equipped with binoculars, telescope and tripod and windproof clothing; some of the fiercest winds to hit Skye strike first at Neist Point.

The two migration periods are especially yielding and bring in such passage birds as purple sandpiper, Manx and sooty shearwaters to augment regular inhabitants like fulmar, kittiwake, herring and common gull, shag, cormorant, eider and long-tailed duck, gannet, razorbill, guillemot, black guillemot, common/Arctic terns, wheatear, meadow and rock pipit, common buzzard, rough-legged buzzard, golden eagle, great northern diver, skuas, and many more.

With little effort you can climb easily from the concrete path to the airy and dramatic top of An t-Aigeach, but do not do this during the breeding season.

Beyond, the path runs on to the lighthouse, where it ends. But you can cross a broad grassy plateau and go down to the very edge of the sea, exploring the rocks and pools, and the small jetty, before ambling back to the starting point.

Any visit to Neist Point is likely to be a wonderful, windswept experience; warm clothing is essential here, even in summer.

145

WALK 4.8:
Healabhal Bheag
(MacLeod's Table South)

This rewarding ascent of the southernmost of the conspicuous MacLeod's Tables avoids the long ascent of its broad East Ridge, preferring to use a path along the northern edge of Gleann Bharcasaig forest before moving on to the hill from the south.

Start/Finish: Orbost. GR.256434.
Distance: 10km (6¼ miles).
Ascent: 475m (1560 feet).

Walk down towards Loch Bharcasaig and follow the track towards the forest. Climb along the edge of the forest and shortly turn west on a path running along its northern edge. When the forest starts dropping to meet the Abhainn Bharcasaig continue, above the line of the burn (using sheep tracks), to reach the remains of a turf dyke across Bealach Bharcasaig.

From the bealach simply climb the hillside to the north, aiming for a prominent bulge of grass and rock. The ascent is quite steep, but not otherwise arduous, and leads to the flat top of the summit, marked by a trig point. The highest point is a small grassy mound at the southern end of the plateau, crossed before reaching the trig.

The table top summit is not as large as its sibling to the north, but it provides a stunning view over Loch Bracadale and to the far Outer Hebrides.

Either return by your outward route, or look for a small cairn a short distance from the trig. From this small cairn follow the edge of the plateau to reach the top of the East Ridge and go down this. The upper section is quite steep and ends at a rock buttress, before the gradient eases off and allows you to savour the view of Loch Bracadale. The buttress can be avoided, on the left, down grass and scree, before returning to the highest part of the descending ridge down which there is an indistinct path.

MacLeod's Tables

For easier going stay as high as possible until, just above the end of the forest, you can cross the hillside to reach the path used on the outward route.

MacLeod's Tables

These curious summits give the appearance of having been chopped off by some ancient giant, and indeed legend claims this was precisely what was done to provide a bed and table for St Columba. In reality their strange formation is down to the horizontal plane of the basalt lavas.

Legend also relates how Healabhal Mhor[1] was indeed used as a table, when Alasdair Crotach, Ninth Chief of the MacLeods and a man who combined the powers of a warrior and the talents of a

---

[1] *Some books suggest that the summit was Healabhal Bheag, but the official version from Dunvegan confirms that it was Healabhal Mhor.*

diplomat, invited taunting lords from the King's Court in Edinburgh to observe how on Skye he had a hall more spacious than that at the King's palace, a roof more lofty, a table more ample and richly laden, and candelabra more ornate. As the Lowland earl arrived he and his retinue were led on to the spacious summit of Healabhal Mhor where the chief had set out an al fresco banquet of meat and wine, illuminated by clansmen holding aloft a ring of torches. Beneath the star-studded heavens, the Lowland lord did indeed graciously admit that the roof was grander, the table more commodious, and the clansmen and their torches more precious than any candelabra. His apology was accepted and the party adjourned to Dunvegan where they were entertained for several days.

WALK 4.9:
Healabhal Mhor
(MacLeod's Table North)

Given the appellation 'mhor' because its flat summit plateau is much larger than that on Healabhal Bheag, the more northerly of MacLeod's Tables is nevertheless lower. Even so, it attracts rather more walkers because of its closer proximity to a convenient road.

Start/Finish: Lay-by on B884, not far from old track leading to Osdale. GR.243464.
Distance: 7km (4½ miles).
Ascent: 455m (1490 feet).

From the lay-by locate a gate giving access to the cart track that leads to two ruined buildings, all that remains of the tiny community of Osdale. As you approach the buildings the track deteriorates to a path. Beyond the crofts go towards a gap in a fence, and continue down to Osdale Burn, which can usually be crossed on stepping stones.

Beyond the burn the path disappears, replaced by intermittent sheep tracks that can be used to cross the heather moorland, heading towards Healabhal Mhor's summit. There is no clear indication of a route, and you need to devise your own, never far from the burn.

Eventually you reach the base of the hill where the slope is more steep. Climb this through continuing heather and the occasional rock band until, finishing steeply, you reach the edge of the flat summit plateau.

There is a good view northwards over Loch Dunvegan, and a broad seascape to the south in which the island of Rhum features prominently.

Return by the same route, taking a bearing on the ruins at Osdale, to be sure of the correct line.

WALK 4.10:
Uiginish Point

Apart from a splendid feeling of isolation, the main reason for finding Uiginish Point is the outstanding view it provides of Dunvegan Castle, and the many off-shore islands in Loch Dunvegan that are frequented by common and grey seals. The walk crosses rough, untracked moorland but is one of the most peaceful places on the Island. A pair of binoculars would be a useful item of equipment on this outing since the islands and the loch are also well populated by birds.

Start/Finish: Uiginish Lodge Hotel. GR.243483 — reached by a minor road from the B884 Glendale road at GR.241465.
Distance: 3km (2 miles).
Ascent: Negligible.

Go through a gate left of the hotel and follow a track through the hotel grounds to join a sheep track across a small hillock, Cnocan Leathan (Broad Hill). More sheep tracks lead you out towards the lighthouse at Uiginish Point.

When you are ready to return, follow the coast round to Ob Dubh (Black Bay), and walk inland from there towards the dilapidated Dun Totaig, rounding Beinn a'Ghuail to return to the hotel starting point.

WALK 4.11:
The Coral Beaches

With more than a passing resemblance on a fine summer's day to a Pacific Island coastline, the Coral Beaches of Claigan are immensely popular, and easy to reach. They are yet another charming feature of this remarkable island, and give immense satisfaction for very little effort.

The start of the walk is reached by driving past the entrance to Dunvegan Castle, and continuing on a single track road past Loch Suardal and Loch Corlarach eventually to reach the isolated farms at Claigan. At a T-junction turn left to a car park.

Start/Finish: Claigan car park. GR.232537.
Distance: 4km (2½ miles).
Ascent: None; unless you climb Cnoc Mor a'Ghrobain
(15m: 50 feet).

Walk down through the car park to a gate giving on to a track that gradually approaches the shore, and passes first around the small bay of Camas Ban. Move right, to reach a wall and follow it to a gap, though you can potter about among the rocks, and simply follow the coastline. Soon you can see the main coral beaches glistening white in the near distance. Cross to the bay, and go round or over Cnoc Mor a'Ghrobain, to reach the end of the peninsula at Groban na Sgeire. How far you can venture out on the exposed lava beds depends on the state of the tide, but the adjoining greensward makes a delightful spot for a picnic.

The off-shore island is Isay, while round to the right lies Lovaig Bay and the cliffs of Sgurr a'Bhagh. Return by your outward route.

Coral Beaches
The fine white sand of the beach is not true coral, but comes from a plant belonging to the red alga (Lithothamnium calcareum). In life this is a rich red colour, but here its calcareous skeleton has been bleached by the sun.

Approaching the Coral Beaches

WALK 4.12:
Lovaig Bay

This walk if extended a short distance is a very long and roundabout way of visiting the Claigan coral beaches, but its main purpose ends at the infrequently-visited Lovaig Bay. The walk is long and is made more difficult late in summer when bracken and heather conceal what little path there is. Further difficulties arise in the form of Bay River, which is tidal, and though not normally a problem to cross, could involve a detour. These minor difficulties aside, the walk is delightful, and provides an opportunity to explore one of the quieter corners of the Island.

Start/Finish: Bay. GR.269539. Follow B886 from Fairy Bridge, and turn down to Bay.
Park, tidily, where the road ends at a U-bend.
Distance: 12km (7½ miles).
Ascent: 60m (200 feet).

Pass through a gate and go down a short road between two houses to reach a green lane through a field running down to the river. The exact line is confusing in summer before the hay crop is taken.

The river slinks along below woodland, but a large cairn marks a good spot to cross it. Follow the true left bank of the river to the southern end of Loch Bay.

If the tide prevents you from reaching the bay do as I did and clamber over a small cliff, or go through a small gate and along the inside of a forest fence round the back of the cliff, though this is rather awkward.

Amble along the shoreline to a narrow path that slips behind a fence and climbs to a small knoll, moving away from the shore. Continue until you reach a ruined building, and pass on to another building on a pleasant grassy shoulder below wooded Sgurr a' Bhagh.

The onward route improves as you approach Rubha Maol where the grassy slopes steepen and drop impressively to the sea. As you round the peninsula Lovaig Bay comes into view with the headland of the Coral Beaches beyond.

If you want to go on to the Coral Beaches you need to detour inland over the cliffs on the far side of Lovaig Bay. You can then continue above the shoreline, ultimately following a wall to Groban na Sgeire and the Coral Beaches beyond.

Return by the same route, remembering to trek over the cliff and into the forest if the tide is in on your return to Bay.

SECTION 5:
Waternish

Of all the promontories of Skye, Waternish (pronounced Vatternish) remains closest to how the Island would have looked centuries ago, when wolves roamed the hillsides and forests, claymores clashed and the battles between the MacLeods and the MacDonalds were a hazard of everyday life. Indeed, the church at Trumpan and Ardmore Bay were the scene of perhaps the bloodiest, most savage clash between the two clans in the Island's history, the Battle of the Spoiling of the Dyke, as it became known (see Walk 5.1).

Little has changed in Waternish; motorised tourists are confined to one road, in and out, compelling those who want to explore to become pedestrians once more. This bent finger of land begins, almost unnoticed, at Fairy Bridge, a seemingly unimportant, cracked, overgrown, and now by-passed, old bridge spanning a tributary burn of Bay River.

Fairy Bridge is the spot where prayer meetings used to be held, a pleasant spot for a picnic, you might think, with lovely views of the surrounding hills and moors. Yet it has an evil reputation, and before prayer meetings were held there only a brave man would pass that way alone after dark, while no horse would cross the bridge, day or night. Some tales suggest that the horses can see the fairies that dwell there dancing on the grassy surrounds, and shy away; others tell of a murder committed there, and of ghosts that prey upon travellers. Certainly two men have been found dead there, at different times. Not surprisingly, the tourist business of Skye has cashed in on the story, and coachloads of visitors are all advised to wish the fairies well as they pass by — just in case! Sadly, that is what this gem of Island folklore has become, an ignominious tourist curiosity.

But, as Jim Crumley emphasises in *The Heart of Skye* it remains 'Fairy Bridge' not 'the Fairy Bridge' or 'the fairy bridge'; it is a bridge, but it is a place, too. And occupied or not by fairies, more than a few take no chances and wave to the fairies in appeasement. Yet, apparently accepted by the fairy community, the landscape of

Waternish has been desecrated by the invasion of power lines destined not solely for the communities of Waternish, but for the population of the Outer Isles, so that they might enjoy the benefits of electric street lighting, refrigerators, television and computers. Such is the Western Isles Connection.

Of the three main peninsulas of northern Skye, Waternish has none of the mountain scenery of Trotternish, and precious little coastal walking to match that of Duirinish. But it remains fine walking country, with most interest set around the margins and southern boundary of the central moorland thrust. Unlike much of the rest of Skye, however, walkers in Waternish must largely fashion their own routes for the region is seldom visited by their kind, and there are no pathways to follow.

The road into Waternish runs up the west coast and ends not far from Trumpan. A little way north, at Sgoir Beag, you can reach the shoreline, but beyond that, as far as Waternish Point, there is nothing but cliffs. Inland (to the peninsula) a scattering of place-names, memorials to long-forgotten battles, brochs, duns and shielings, are all that now tell of former times.

Today the communities that remain cling to the edges of this almost isolated land. The moors are barren, abandoned to Nature's kind, yet seamed with history and the threads of island culture that weave a tapestry of intrigue, mystery and timelessness. Dun Borrafiach is one of the most attractive duns on Skye, built with enormous blocks of stone, and though Dun Gearymore a short distance away has survived less well, it remains worthy of exploration.

In a creek near Waternish Point Prince Charlie and Flora MacDonald rested for a while on the Prince's journey from South Uist to Skye in 1746. Having tried unsuccessfully to land at Ardmore, where they were fired on by soldiers, they sailed around Waternish Point before crossing Loch Snizort to land at a place called Allt a'Chuain in Kilbride Bay, about 1km (½ mile) south-west of Mogstadt House.

From Hallin a narrow road cuts across the peninsula to the twin villages of Geary and Gillen, neatly arranged, or so it seems from a distance, along the top of the cliffs above Loch Snizort, while an old track crosses from Waternish House to Loch Losait, the first place

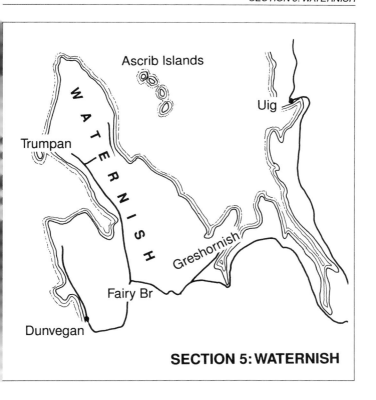

SECTION 5: WATERNISH

south of Waternish Point where access to the shoreline is feasible. South of this more cliffs run on to Loch Diubaig, where the waters of Loch Snizort probe the land to create two smaller peninsulas, those of Greshornish and Lyndale.

Inland from Fairy Bridge lies Beinn Chreagach, the highest point of Waternish, and Beinn na Boineide. Dedicated moorland wanderers will find their untamed, untramped company eminently acceptable. Seekers of solitude and the opportunity to wander quietly will find Waternish just the corner of heaven its inhabitants always knew it was.

WALK 5.1:
Ardmore Point

Today in many a clachan in the Isle of Mists and rain
They tell at winter ceilidh this story o'er again
And many a timid cailleach, when the evening shadows fall,
Avoids the place that bears the name 'Destruction of the Wall'.

The Songs of Skye: The Burning of Trumpan Church

Trumpan Church lies well up the western coast of Waternish, reached from Fairy Bridge along the B886 and the single track road to Ardmore. Ardmore Point is the place where Prince Charlie and Flora MacDonald attempted to alight on his crossing from South Uist, and would have done so had they not been fired on by the soldiers stationed there. This brief walk wanders out to one of the most evocative spots on the Island, around the sheltering embrace of Ardmore Bay.

Start/Finish: Car park opposite Trumpan Church. GR.225613.
Distance: 3km (2 miles).
Ascent: Negligible.

Go down the hill from the church and follow a cart track on the right. Almost immediately, at a gap in a wall, cross to a path, trending right. Continue down the path to a fence, following it and then crossing it to pursue the curve of a small bay. Black boulders and tangles of dark brown seaweed form the beach, washed by waters from which seals gaze at you curiously.

The path climbs Ard Beag and descends to another bay before climbing above a natural arch and pressing on to Ardmore Point. At Millegearraidh you pass the site of the Battle of the Spoiling of a Dyke. From the Point there are fine views of the small islands of Clett, Mingay and Isay, and the cliffs on the west side of Loch Bay.

Follow a narrow path above the shoreline of Ardmore Bay past Ardmore House, where a broad track is encountered, heading back around the shoreline to rejoin your outward route beyond a gate.

The Battle of the Spoiling of a Dyke

On a Sunday in May 1578 a party of MacDonalds from Uist landed in Ardmore Bay in a fleet of eight ships under cover of mist, and found their way to Trumpan Church where they surprised the local people, MacLeods, at worship. In one of the cruellest episodes in the Island's history, the MacDonalds set fire to the thatched church, burning the congregation or putting any that escaped the flames to the sword, save one. The woman, mortally wounded, escaped and raised the alarm, though the flames of the church had been seen by the guards at Dunvegan Castle. Vengeance was swift, for the MacLeods, aided by the forces of the Fairy Flag, that changed "the very grass blades...to armed men", set about the MacDonalds, forced them back to the bay, where they discovered that their galleys had been beached by a retreating tide. All but a handful of the MacDonalds were slain, and their bodies laid alongside a stone dyke that was pushed over them as a makeshift grave.

The MacDonalds' act was itself a reprisal for an equally savage act, when the MacLeods found hundreds of them hiding in a cave on the island of Eigg, and suffocated them by lighting a fire at the cave entrance.

Sceptics might wonder at this tale. No one disputes that there was a battle, though some authorities maintain it was at a different Battle of Waternish that the Fairy Flag was unfurled.

Likewise, records show that Waternish at the time belonged to the MacLeods of Lewis, not of Skye, who did not attain possession until 30 years after the date of the massacre. Nor is there any mention among the works of contemporary writers to the Massacre of Eigg. And would the MacLeods have pushed a perfectly good wall, used as protection for crops, over slain bodies when they could just as easily have dumped them in the sea? Finally, in what circumstances would a sea-faring clan like the MacDonalds of Uist be likely to overlook the consequences of a retreating tide?

As is typical of Skye, here again we encounter elements of the Island's history so strongly permeated with tradition and mangled in the telling by the passage of time as to defy logical explanation. Nor should we be too diligent in seeking one.

Lady Grange

In the graveyard at Trumpan Church lies Lady Grange, who died insane in 1745, following the heartless treatment by her husband, James Erskine, Lord Grange, a senator of the College of Justice and a brother of the Earl of Mar, who raised the Jacobite Rebellion of 1715. Afraid that Lady Grange was a government spy and would divulge his connivance in Jacobite plots, her husband abducted her and after carrying her first to Moidart and then to Heisker off North Uist, finally imprisoned her for seven years on the island of St Kilda. On this remote Atlantic island she was among folk whose language she did not know, and who did not speak English. She was, by all accounts, a refined, intelligent and beautiful woman though "cursed with a congenital irascibility of temper, bordering at times on insanity" and given to drinking. Finally, friends having discovered her whereabouts, she was brought to Skye, where she was at first confined to a cave near Idrigill Point in Duirinish, before being allowed a certain measure of freedom until death brought an end to her miseries.

The truth of this story was described by Boswell as "frightfully romantic as if it had been the fiction of a gloomy fancy". Yet even in her death the story of Lady Grange did not end, for, while a coffin of sods was consigned to a grave in Duirinish, her body was brought for burial to the ancient churchyard at Trumpan. It was not the first time that she had been represented by a coffin filled with sods, for her initial disappearance was explained by the announcement of her death, and her 'interment' in the churchyard of Greyfriars in Edinburgh.

WALK 5.2:
Unish and Waternish Point

The northern point of Waternish has a feeling of remoteness and natural order that few regions of Skye possess; it is not a malign feeling, but one of a place untouched by the passage of time. Throughout there is a strong feeling of going back into history, supported by

The monument to Roderick MacLeod, who died in the second battle of Waternish, c.1530.

the remains of man's past presence here, and the walk is one of the most relaxing and peaceful outings on Skye.

The walk, which reaches the unmanned light at Waternish Point, makes use of a good vehicle track before continuing along the cliff top to the Point. You can extend the walk a little by following the track to the ruined crofts at Unish.

Start/Finish: Trumpan Church. GR.225613.
Distance: 13km (8 miles).
Ascent: 240m (790 feet).

From the car park opposite the church go left along the narrow road until it turns sharp right, and here go left through a gate (No dogs allowed) on to a broad track that leads out across a great spread of heather moorland, a broad sweep of purple countryside in late summer and early autumn. You pass through another gate before finally breaking out into magnificent, windswept curlew country.

As you go there are a number of interesting historical detours to fill the time. A large cairn on the moor on the right, is a memorial to John MacLeod, who fell in the second battle of Waternish around 1530. Further on, a beehive-shaped memorial on a hill on the left (easily accessible) commemorates Roderick MacLeod, his son, who died in the same battle, such was the sad and often senseless loss of life during the times of the clan battles. Both cairns were thoughtfully restored by an American branch of the Clan MacLeod in 1985.

Further along the track you find two brochs. The first, Dun Borrafiach, used unusually large stones in its construction, and was certainly one of the most well-constructed brochs on the Island. The second dun, more ruinous and a little closer to the trail, is Dun Gearymore. From both there would have been excellent views of any approaching marauders.

Beyond Dun Gearymore the path turns north-east and heads for the ruined crofts at Unish. Finding your way down to the unmanned light from Unish is not difficult, but likely to be very wet after rain.

Alternatively, you can leave the track at the point where it changes direction), and go left to reach the coastline near An Camastac, from there following the excellent coastline, with good views to the Outer Isles, up to the Point.

Although it is feasible to continue around the coastline to reach Geary, the going is considerably more arduous. There is no track to help you along, and the terrain is of the roughest kind. In view of this, the wisest way back is by your outward route.

WALK 5.3:
Beinn an Sguirr
and the Waternish Forest

This interesting and varied walk divides cleanly into two halves; the first section follows a good trail through woodland inhabited by red deer, while the second part crosses the upper escarpment of Beinn an Sguirr high above Loch Snizort. The former is easy walking, but the latter, though following a narrow path throughout, comes close to some spectacular and unstable cliffs high above Loch Losait.

Start/Finish: Small parking space about 250m/yds before road end at Gillen. GR.268594.
Distance: 5½km (3½ miles).
Ascent: 220m (725 feet).

Go past the cottages at Gillen and through a gate on to a track to another gate. Keep ahead, ignoring a left turn, and soon enter a forest of mixed pine. The broad forest trail climbs gently and merges with another trail, there reaching the edge of the forest, now with trees only on the left.

At a prominent junction, turn left between wooden gateposts (the on-going trail leads to Waternish House), and continue along a broad track, ascending gradually. On the way you pass a small shooting range before the trail traverses open moorland to cross a broad ridge extending north from Beinn Charnach Bheag.

Once across the ridge the trail gently descends with fine views on the right over lower woodland to the hills of Trotternish. Just after the descending trail bends to the right look for a small cairn on the left, beside the trail. Here leave the trail on a narrow trod through banks of heather. This path, though not always easy to follow, does accompany you the rest of the way to the track running down to Loch Losait.

A short distance further on, at a low turf dyke, you reach the eastern edge of the Beinn an Sguirr escarpment, a surprising and dramatic moment, the dyke proving to be a comfortable and well-placed spot for a rest. The continuing path now follows the escarpment, circumventing a number of steep gullies, all of which require a safe distance.

The views are spectacular both of the immediate surrounds and across Loch Snizort to the Ascrib Islands, Uig Bay, and the northern hills of Trotternish. As Loch Losait's dark beach comes into view, so, too, you encounter impressive intrusive dykes in the basaltic cliffs, like rocky ladders running up the cliffs.

Eventually the escarpment peters out as the path approaches the forest edge once more. There are difficult and messy ways through the forest, but by keeping it always on your left, and following the perimeter, you finally reach a collapsed stone and turf dyke and the track to Loch Losait, known locally as Score Bay.

All that remains is to turn left and follow the access track back to rejoin your outward route beside the second gate.

WALK 5.4:
Greshornish Point

This circuit of the wild, remote and infrequently-visited Greshornish peninsula is simple and delightful, suitable for a day when motivation is long on eventually and short on now! With a certain amount of diligence you can detect a narrow path all the way round, rather better on the west coast than on the east, though it is scarcely needed.

Projecting like a stubby finger into the far greater Loch Snizort, Greshornish is flanked on the west by diminutive Loch Diubaig, and on the east by Loch Greshornish.

Loch Greshornish, which extends southwards to the community of Edinbane, is now used for commercial salmon farming. At various times, however, the loch is claimed to have seen icebergs, walruses, and a visitation of sharks so great in number that no one would summon the courage to swim in the loch. These days you are more likely to encounter quizzical seals.

Start/Finish: Road bend 100m/yds past entrance to Greshornish House Hotel. GR.341541.
Very limited parking; do not cause obstruction.
Distance: 6km (3¾ miles).
Ascent: Nominal; many undulations.

From the road bend go left through a gate on to a broad access track curving towards a large stand of trees. As the trees are approached, the path forks. The right branch leads to farm buildings, and will be your way back, so, go left to a gate beyond which a grassy path leads across to Loch Diubaig. Out in Loch Snizort the Ascrib Islands look much closer than they are.

From the inlet of Loch Diubaig a series of linking sheep tracks leads north-eastwards around the peninsula, some passing very close to the edge of high cliffs. Maol na h-Airde, the highest point along the peninsula, is worth the token and almost unavoidable struggle to reach its cairned summit, for it has a fine outlook, with a good view of the entire peninsula and that of its neighbour Lyndale across Loch Greshornish.

Continuing to make the most of sheep tracks where necessary, press on to the surprisingly level greensward at Camas Lagan before finally reaching Greshornish Point. From here you gaze out to the low islands of Eilean Mór and Eilean Beag, which are popular with seals.

The sheep tracks continue down the east coast, where you soon reach the well-positioned Dun na h-Airde, its main entrance still clearly evident. More sheep tracks lead on, back towards Greshornish House Hotel, the position of which is betrayed by its ring of trees. As you approach the end of the walk you meet a wall, to the left of which a wire fence runs down to the loch. Cross neither the wall nor the fence, but turn right, along the line of the wall, and follow it and a half-hearted path up to the right of the old farm buildings (renovated in 1995) not far from the stand of trees at which the track forked on the outward journey. Pass the buildings on the right, and then turn left to follow the track back to your starting point.

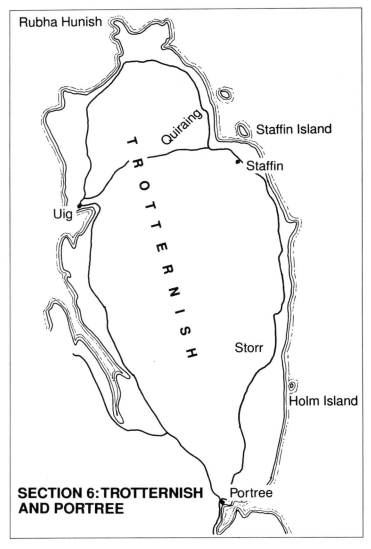

**SECTION 6: TROTTERNISH
AND PORTREE**

SECTION 6:
Trotternish and Portree

Trotternish is the largest of the northern peninsulas of Skye, and, at Rubha Hunish, includes the most northerly point on the Island. If Skye was turned on its head, and Trotternish therefore more accessible than the Cuillin, it would be considerably more popular than it is among the walking fraternity, for it contains excellent walking country, the longest continuous ridge on the Island, and scenery that is every bit as dramatic and bizarre as the Cuillin.

The whole peninsula is encircled by a good road, though only one road succeeds in crossing the main thrust of the ridge, from Staffin to Uig, via the Bealach Ollasgairte. The coastline is also splendid, and boasts vertiginous sea cliffs, sea stacks, caves, natural arches and waterfalls.

The central part of the peninsula takes the form of the Trotternish Ridge, a splendid long distance walk that contains more than a dozen separate summits, most of excellent green turf and ideal for walking. The complete traverse of the ridge is a major undertaking, but sufficient points of access exist along its length to enable the ridge to be tackled piecemeal. The highest point of the ridge is The Storr, a place better renowned for the curious arrangements of pinnacles in the sanctuary below its cliffs, among which the Old Man, The Needle and Church Rock are especially imposing. The pinnacles of the Storr sanctuary are particularly well seen from the vicinity of Loch Fada and Loch Leathan, two large lochs that are popular with anglers. Another loch, Loch Mealt, lies beside the road nearer to Staffin, and close to one of Skye's most outstanding landforms, Kilt Rock. The upper part of the cliffs at this point is vertical black columnar basalt, while the lower consists of horizontal oolite beds that alternate white and grey. The overall impression is very realistically that of an enormous kilt.

Amid the vast greenness of Trotternish you also gain another impression, that of a landscape stripped bare of trees: although not entirely true, long years receiving the attentions of cattle and sheep have removed large areas of juvenile woodland. Sufficient remains, however, in every steep-sided ravine, on loch-encircled islands, and among the crevices on the cliffs, to demonstrate that Skye was once a well-wooded country, bearing large stands of birch, rowan, willow, aspen, hazel and oak.

At the northern end of the ridge lies another outstanding collection of rock oddities in a region known as The Quiraing, formed by massive landslips in the layers of basalt lavas of which the area is composed.

Flodigarry, north of Staffin, was the home between 1750 and 1772 of Flora MacDonald, before she and her husband Captain Allan MacDonald moved to Kingsburgh, where they were visited by Johnson and Boswell, who found her to be "a woman of middle stature, soft features, gentle manners, and elegant presence".

Duntulm Castle, now in ruins but undoubtedly at one time an imposing castle, was the stronghold of the MacDonalds from about 1539, though the exact date is not known. Much of the castle was built by Sir Donald Gorme MacDonald of Sleat on the orders of King James VI, who instructed him to "make his residence and duelling at Duntillum, and, yf he has not a sufficient comelie house ansuerable to his estate alreddy thair, that he sall with all convenient diligence prepair materiallis and cause build ane civil and comelie house, and, yf his house be decayit, that he sall repair and mend the same". Among a list of other kingly requirements, the chief was instructed to limit his consumption of wine to 4 tuns a year (1008 gallons, or almost 11000 present-day bottles!).

Duntulm Castle lies on a promontory at the northern end of Score Bay, while at the southern end stands the scattered community of Kilmuir, where Flora MacDonald lies buried. Close by, one of Skye's 'black houses' has been reconditioned, and others built on the site of what is now a fine museum of Skye life. The lands of Kilmuir were described by Thomas Pennant in 1772 as "laughing with corn", a reference to the quality of corn produced in a region that was always bitterly contested by the MacDonalds and the MacLeods.

Before reaching the shelter of Uig Bay, the Trotternish road slips by Monkstadt, where Prince Charlie found brief sanctuary after landing on Skye from the Outer Isles on 29 June 1746. Finally, in a mighty flourish the road drops quickly to Uig Bay, whence ferries convey passengers to the Outer Isles. Beyond, from Uig to

Kingsburgh, the road is one of the oldest on Skye, formerly a bridleway, which, following a government survey in 1799, was turned into a road with the intention of opening up the Island.

Once the end of Loch Snizort is passed the road completes its circle of Trotternish, striking across country, past the straggling township of Borve, to Portree.

WALK 6.1:
Hunish and Meall Tuath

The most northerly point of the Island is Rubha Hunish, a long, grassy headland ringed by crags and fine sea stacks, but it is not easy to reach, defended from the rest of the Island by the craggy northern face of Meall Tuath, through which there is only one way, and this is difficult to find. Meall Tuath nevertheless is a worthy objective for a walk and is a splendid viewpoint.

Start/Finish: Parking space for Duntulm Castle. GR.411741.
Distance: 7km (4½ miles).
Ascent: 210m (695 feet).

From the roadside parking place Duntulm Castle is reached in a matter of minutes along an obvious and signposted track above Score Bay.

The castle was the MacDonald base on Skye from the early sixteenth century, and has a long and chequered history that embraces both glory and bloodshed. Little remains of the original structure, and what does is under restoration. At the entrance to the castle is a large memorial to the MacArthurs, hereditary pipers to the MacDonalds.

A path from the castle leads around Port Duntulm, northwards along the shore of Tulm Bay. When you are forced upwards, away from the bay, aim directly for the top of Meall Tuath.

Meall Tuath has a second top, south-west of the highest point, and between the two you will find a rocky path slipping down to the headland below. If you cannot find it, content yourself with perching bravely on Meall Tuath, savouring the ever-present breezes, and scanning the waves for passing birdlife, a visiting whale or curious seal.

Duntulm Castle

The castle occupies a formidable position on a small promontory to the north of Score Bay and is virtually inaccessible from the sea, except through Port Duntulm bay.

There is a local tradition that the site was occupied by a fort from very early times, which was demolished to provide material for the castle. For most of the time the castle was in the possession of the MacLeods of Dunvegan, but it is generally accepted that the MacDonalds moved here from Dun Sgathaich around 1539. Certainly, they were in residence when James V paid them a visit in 1540.

Two views are proffered for the MacDonalds' final departure from Duntulm. One concerns the tragedy that befell the family of Donald Gorm when a child fell from its nurse's arms over the battlements, to be dashed to death on the rocks below — the luckless nurse was subsequently cast adrift in a boat full of holes, though some aver that friends hid her in the castle until it was safe for her to be moved away, casting a dummy adrift in the boat instead. The second tale revolves around the disturbingly frequent bacchanalian visitations of the ghost of Donald Gorm Mor, who sought to return to his earthly home, and preferred his Clan brew to the ambrosia of the gods.

It is traditionally thought the MacDonalds left Duntulm just before the Rebellion of 1715, though there is evidence that they were still in residence ten years later. But as to the exact date, we are ignorant.

WALK 6.2:
Loch Sneosdal
and Creag Sneosdal

The Stygian waters of Loch Sneosdal lie in austere repose directly beneath Creag Sneosdal, the northern escarpment of Suidh a'Mhinn (sic). Much of the terrain within which Loch Sneosdal lies is wet and generally uninteresting, though this walk makes use of a good track that goes within a short distance of the loch. Beyond that it tackles steep grassy slopes, up and down, to give a fairly demanding walk of short duration.

At the northern end of the Heribusta road, at Peingown, are both Flora MacDonald's grave and an interesting museum of life on Skye displayed in a series of original and reconstructed croft cottages.

Start/Finish: Sharp bend on Kilvaxter-Heribusta road, off A855. GR.395701.
Distance: 6km (3¾ miles).
Ascent: 265m (870 feet).

Pass through a gate near the road bend and follow a track to a building on the right, beyond which the track is no longer surfaced. It continues, however, as a firm cart track, heading for Creag Sneosdal, conspicuous by an intrusive dyke in the cliff face.

The track wanders across the moorland, and when it finally expires continue by aiming for the left edge of the cliff, across a short stretch of rough moorland, which soon brings you to Loch Sneosdal. Anyone not seeking to complete the round of the cliffs above should simply retrace their steps from this point.

Otherwise, ascend a steep grassy slope beyond the loch to reach the top of the cliff. Good, close-cropped turf leads you up past a great gully that divides the cliff, and provides a dramatic view of the loch below. As you approach the highest point, you encounter a fence along the cliff edge. It is debatable whether the trig pillar a short distance away marks the highest point of Suidh a'Mhinn; there does seem to be marginally higher ground near the cliffs.

Follow the fence until you are beyond the western end of the cliff, and at a fence junction descend along the northern side of a second fence, aiming for the angle in a turf dyke below. Walk along the line of the dyke until it changes direction, and from there head for a group of sheep enclosures from where you can reach the outward cart track.

WALK 6.3:
Loch Harsco
and the Northern Quiraing

Beyond the far northern end of the Trotternish Ridge lie flat moors and the wide expanse of The Minch, but before the landslip sculptings of the Quiraing finally cease it is possible to visit them from the north, by a much less frequented route.

Start/Finish: Flodigarry, near start of cart track to Loch Langaig. GR.464710. Limited roadside parking.
Distance: 6km (3¾ miles).
Ascent: 315m (1035 feet).

Set off along the cart track and almost immediately you meet Loch Langaig, from where you have a fine view of the craggy profile of Leac nan Fionn ahead. The track skirts the loch and diminishes to a path as it works its way to secluded Loch Hasco, set in a fine situation at the base of the steep hillside below the cliffs of Leac nan Fionn's east face.

Near Loch Harsco, the path meets a fence, beyond which it slips through heather banks into a deep grassy hollow. Go across the hollow only to meet another one, this time bouldery, and crossed by contouring around one side. Before long the path swings left and into the midst of the pinnacles and crags of the Quiraing, which can be explored at your leisure, before retracing your steps.

WALK 6.4:
The Quiraing

Formed in post-glacial times when underlying sedimentary rocks could no longer sustain the weight of the heavier overlying lavas and as a result moved eastwards in a series of massive and spectacular landslips, the amazing formations of the Quiraing are among the most popular places to visit on Skye. Lying to the east of the rounded Meall na Suiramach, of which it would once have formed part, the Quiraing is best reached from Bealach Ollasgairte, where the east-facing escarpment of the Trotternish Ridge is breached by the Staffin-Uig road. Days of poor visibility are not suited to the exploration of this natural maze, an immensely popular place with early tourists, and just as much so today.

How far you explore will depend on your ability (there is moderate rock scrambling in a few places) and on your willingness to climb unstable and steep slopes of grass, earth and boulders. For many it will be reward enough simply to wander among the amazing rock formations.

Start/Finish: Parking area at Bealach Ollasgairte (not named on maps). GR.440679.
Distance: Variable: 4km (2½ miles).
Ascent: Nominal.

The route into the heart of the Quiraing is almost level, and sets off from the Bealach Ollasgairte through a short stretch of (usually) boggy ground before settling down into a narrow and quite exhilarating, almost alpine, crossing below the cliffs of Maoladh Mor, and past Cnoc a'Mheirlich.

Beyond an easy gully you turn a corner to be faced with the magnificent sight of the massive cliffs of Meall na Suiramach and, opposite, the imposing wedge of rock known as The Prison, vertiginous cliffs on one side and very steep grassy banks on the other; this is not an objective for inexperienced walkers or idle curiosity.

Stay on a path leading to a cairn on a small bealach at the northern end of The Prison, from where you get a good view of the next wonder of this amazing place, The Needle. By climbing a slope and going left to the base of the rocks you can then pass around the back of The Needle. Keep going across a grassy slope to a gap between two towers beyond which you gain access to the third of the Quiraing's surprises, The Table. You need to clamber up a short gully to reach a natural, but dry, moat that surrounds The Table. You

Walking in the Quiraing

The Prison, Quiraing

can reach the top of The Table, a large, flat area of close-cropped grass, by a steep, grassy slope. Once on top, simply explore, and enjoy the whole spectacular scene.

Because of the complexities of the terrain within the Quiraing, the safest course is to retrace your steps, but only after exploring more of this fascinating landscape. Do not be lured into attempting to climb on to Meall na Suiramach; there are no feasible routes at this point.

WALK 6.5:
Meall na Suiramach

Meall na Suiramach is the parent mountain from which the pinnacles of the Quiraing are fashioned. Its ascent is easy, and though it is never likely to usurp the popularity of the Quiraing, a gentle ascent of this rounded, grassy hill is not without its attractions, especially on a clear day. There is no point, and an element of danger, in doing this walk in poor visibility.

Start/Finish: Parking area at Bealach Ollasgairte (not named on maps). GR.440679.
Distance: 3km (2 miles).
Ascent: 295m (965 feet).

From the parking area strike across the moor on to the shoulder of Maoladh Mor, always taking the easiest and driest line before the gradient eases, and you can stroll beside a line of wooden posts to the trig pillar on the highest point.

Because the top of the hill is not perched directly above the Quiraing, you need to walk towards the cliff edge (with care) for a stunning view of the labyrinthine landscape below.

If you elect to return along the escarpment edge be sure to remain well above the cliffs as you recross Maoladh Mor.

WALK 6.6:
The Storr Sanctuary

The climb to the Storr Sanctuary, within which are gathered a most unique assortment of pinnacles, is both strenuous and worthwhile. There can be few red-blooded walkers who are not sufficiently inspired by the weird arrangement of towers when viewed from the Trotternish road to make the effort of visiting the amazing arena in which they stand.

Pathways through the forest begin from a convenient parking place just off the road, but for years they have been totally impassable and bedevilled by deep, clutching bogs. Repair work is in hand, but it will be some years before the ascent through the forest regains its composure. Meanwhile, do not use the forest trails; give them time to breathe. The information panel adjoining the car park will tell you when the paths are ready for use.

The parking place remains the most convenient spot to leave your car, from where you walk down the road to the southern edge of the forest. Off-road parking near the start of the walk is very limited.

Start/Finish: Car park, off A855. GR.509529.
Distance: 3km (2 miles).
Ascent: 325m (1065 feet).

Walk down the road to the southernmost edge of the forest, and cross a stile over a boundary fence that allows you to access a broad stretch of ground between the forest (right) and a dyke (an old boundary wall). Climb this steep strip of ground to the top edge of the forest, where you can follow the forest boundary round to reach the Storr Sanctuary. There is a path through the forest, starting a short way along the forest edge, but this is often very wet and impassable, and should be avoided.

Outside the boundary wall and above the forest you are on active crofting land, used for grazing sheep: any dogs you may have must be kept on a lead at all times.

The principal feature of interest in The Sanctuary is the shapely

The Storr

obelisk, The Old Man of Storr, undercut at the base and seeming to defy gravity and the might of the Skye weather. It stands 50m (165 feet) high and was first climbed by the late Don Whillans in 1955 by a route still graded Very Severe — looking at the way the rock overhangs you may wonder, how? or why?

Other weird pinnacles, however, vie for your attention, especially The Needle, a bizarre slab of apparently unsupported rock from which blocks of rock have fallen to create two 'eyes'. Nor is it only the pinnacles that amaze, for the whole amphitheatre of The Sanctuary is a fascinating place of exploration, backed by seemingly impregnable dark cliffs that rise sharply to The Storr itself, the highest summit along the Trotternish Ridge.

For an outstanding view of the whole scene you need to climb beyond Needle Rock to higher ground, then about face to see the pinnacles set against Loch Leathan and the distant purple form of the Red Cuillin and mainland peaks.

To vary the return, descend to the northern edge of the forest and turn left, down the north-eastern forest fence to reach a gate by the road, not far from the car park.

175

WALK 6.7:
The Storr

The Storr is the highest point of the Trotternish Ridge, and the place where the dramatic land-slipped scenery for which the ridge is famous, begins. The complete ridge traverse is a major undertaking, but each of the principal summits can be attacked from at least one direction, and The Storr is no exception.

This ascent, which takes you through The Sanctuary, is a strenuous and interesting walk, but uses eroded slopes to reach the main ridge. It is not advised in poor visibility.

Start/Finish: Car park, off A855. GR.509529.
Distance: 6½km (4 miles).
Ascent: 570m (1870 feet).

Follow Walk 6.4 into The Sanctuary, go behind the Old Man and along the path above The Needle, which crosses the hillside below the cliffs of The Storr. As the cliffs reduce in height, so you reach a grassy bealach. Cross a fence, and then turn past the top of a gully descending towards Loch Scamadal into the shallow basin of Coire Scamadal. Now ascend along the edge of the cliffs towards the summit, a tiring plod up eroded slopes penetrated by the dramatic gullies of the main Storr cliff. The ground near the gullies and along the edge is friable and unstable, and should not be approached too closely.

As the top of the slope is reached you cross below a barrier of rocks on the right that guards the summit plateau, before using a grassy corridor through them to gain the top.

If retracing your steps, note that the grassy route through the rock band is marked by a cairn, and continue down to the lowest point of the shallow corrie, directly above the Scamadal cliffs, from where the path goes right, leading back into The Sanctuary.

On a fine day, an alternative finish goes south, down grassy slopes to the Bealach Beag, marked by a cairn. Note that the bealach is distinguished by a very marked easing of the gradient. On the way to it you will need to avoid both the top of a major gully and a boulder gully that sends its rubbish into Coire Faoin.

From the Bealach Beag follow the left bank of a small burn which finds a way through the escarpment by way of a small easy gully. Descend this, and then follow a path which you will see crossing the moor. This is invariably wet, but is the quickest way back down to the road.

WALK 6.8:
The Trotternish Ridge

The distance from Ben Dearg to Meall na Suiramach by raven is almost 20km (12 miles), on foot the distance rises to 28½km (18 miles), something with which only the strongest of walkers are likely to feel comfortable. That distance can be reduced a little by omitting Meall na Suiramach (-3½km: 2 miles), and finishing at the Bealach Ollasgairte (to which transport will have to be arranged), and by omitting the brief detour to bag Ben Dearg (-2½km: 1½ miles). The minimum distance required for the traverse is therefore 22½km (14 miles). Most walkers include Ben Dearg, but finish when the Bealach Ollasgairte is reached (25km: 15½ miles).

Experienced backpackers will have no difficulty coming to terms with the logistics of this trip, indeed, such an approach spanning two days, and involving a high camp along the way, will make them the major beneficiaries of the spectacular walking and outstanding views the ridge has to offer. The mid-point is around the Bealach na Leacaich, between Flasvein and Creag a'Lain.

Start: Lay-by (small parking area) on A655. GR.495509.
Finish: Bealach Ollasgairte. GR.440679.
Distance: 28½km (18 miles).
Ascent: 2100m (6890 feet).

From the parking place, which is near a bend in the road, follow the nearby burn inland over rough ground, and climb steeply to reach Bealach Mor.

177

Walkers undertaking the full traverse should go left (south-west) here to start on Ben Dearg. The approach is easy, but finishes up a short stretch of rocky and bouldery ground.

From Bealach Mor, go north-east over two minor bumps to cross Bealach Beag (cairn), and from there ascend the grassy southern slopes of The Storr. From the summit bear west of north, keeping above Coire Scamadal, to descend to the Bealach a'Chuirn, from where a steep climb takes you on to Hartaval, the second highest summit in Trotternish.

Beyond Hartaval you press on, gently undulating across the Bealach Hartaval, climbing over broken rocks on to Sgurr a'Mhalaidh and Baca Ruadh, a fine vantage point overlooking Coir' an t-Seasgaich. Between Baca Ruadh and Flasvein the escarpment is rather convoluted and pierced by deep gullies that should be avoided. Go first to the promontory-like Sgurr a'Mhadaidh Ruadh before crossing to Creag a'Lain, across the Bealach na Leacaich and up to Flasvein.

After Flasvein, the ridge narrows and marches on across Bealach Chaiplin, Groba nan Each, Bealach Amadal, Beinn Mheadhonach and Bealach a'Mhoramhain to Beinn Edra, a fine summit due east of Glen Uig, from which it is often ascended independently.

North of Beinn Edra, the ridge turns to cross Bealach Uige, Druim na Coille and Bealach nan Coisichean, before ascending fairly steeply to Biode Buidhe, the final summit before the long, easy descent to the Bealach Ollasgairte, and the road. Beyond that, for purists, lies the grassy mound of Meall na Suiramach, a final ascent that those who have traversed the ridge in a single day may be forgiven for omitting. Alternatively, you may elect to finish the ridge walk by heading straight into the labyrinthine Quiraing.

WALK 6.9:
Biode Buidhe

This brief walk nevertheless affords a tantalising glimpse of the great Trotternish Ridge, and the clifftop view of the landslip formations below the long escarpment. It is grassy throughout, and can usually be accomplished in lightweight walking shoes.

Start/Finish: Parking area at Bealach Ollasgairte (not named on maps). GR.440679.
Distance: 3km (2 miles).
Ascent: 215m (705 feet).

Little is needed in the way of route description since you can almost see the top of the hill from your starting point. Simply leave the parking space at the bealach, and walk southwards, gradually ascending the grassy slopes on an improving path. Take great care in the vicinity of the escarpment edge.

The summit gives a bird's-eye view of the isolated lump of Cleat and its attendant lochs. Return by the same route.

WALK 6.10:
Beinn Edra

This delightful approach to the Trotternish Ridge comes from the west, via Glen Uig, and ascends through a landscape less dramatic but just as fascinating as that beyond the ridge. Here there are fine waterfalls and a wealth of birdlife to keep you company.

Glen Uig scythes into the moorland slopes almost to the foot of Beinn Edra, and roads run into the glen on both the north and south side. A strange landscape of small hillocks, known as the 'fairy hills' has earned the glen the title 'Fairy Glen'.

This approach climbs to the Bealach a'Mhoramhain, and the possibility exists to continue across Beinn Edra to the Bealach Uige, and descend from there to the crag-edged moorland fringe above Balnaknock. This, however, involves some burn crossing, and the awkward circumvention of a number of penetrating ravines where the potential for error and a slip outweighs the undoubted pleasure of devising a circular walk.

Start/Finish: Balnaknock, Glen Uig. GR.419628. Leave the A856 on the single track road signposted to Sheader. There is limited parking space in a lay-by at Balnaknock, just before the last house.
Distance: 11km (7 miles).
Ascent: 490m (1610 feet).

From the lay-by walk past the last house for a short distance and go through a gate on the right giving access to a wide track. After another gate, walk on until the track meets the Lon an t-Sratha, and find a suitable place to cross. There are a number of convenient boulders, but some of these may be submerged if the burn is in spate and you may have to detour for a short distance. Once across, continue with the cart track beside the burn, until finally it peters out.

Keeping much to the same direction (east) cross the trackless, hummocky moorland (boggy, but usually avoidable, in places) until you reach the delightful falls on the Abhainn Dhubh. Cross the burn and a subsidiary burn, and head north across a rough, untracked hillside until you meet a turf dyke above a band of rocks.

Beyond the rocks follow the dyke which continues in a very direct way to the Bealach Mhoramhain, where you join the main Trotternish Ridge. Turn left here and walk up easy slopes of close-cropped grass and moss to the cairn on Beinn Edra, and its outstanding view.

Take particular care near the cliff edge if the wind is strong from the west. The towers of the Quiraing can be seen above Staffin Bay to the north, matched by those of The Storr Sanctuary to the south. Far to the east on a good day you can pick out the blue hills of Sutherland and Wester Ross.

WALK 6.11:
Sgurr a'Mhadaidh Ruaidh
and Baca Ruadh

Both these summits project from the main Trotternish Ridge in a bold and challenging way, between them forming the high Coir' an t-Seasgaich. **Their ascent is not an easy undertaking, and should only be considered by experienced walkers in conditions of good visibility.** The walk involves a good dose of trackless moorland wandering and a very steep grassy slope, and will appeal to walkers who can master the characteristic ruggedness of this Skye terrain.

> **Start/Finish:** Lealt. GR.507608. Leave the A855 shortly after crossing the Lealt River.
> **Distance:** 12km (7½ miles).
> **Ascent:** 645m (2115 feet).

Beyond Lealt, where parking is limited, it is possible to drive along a rough cart track to the vicinity of Loch Cuithir, and this will save 6km (3¾ miles) overall, but it is extremely rough. By using the large lay-by near the Inver Tote waterfalls (GR.516605), and walking along the quiet lane to Lealt, you add 2km (1¼ miles), but enjoy better parking without the risk of damaging your car.

The road in to Loch Cuithir was constructed to exploit the diatomite deposits in Loch Cuithir, which had many industrial uses. This involved draining the original Loch Cuithir, and what you see today is a shadow of its former self, though Nature has clawed back some of its original atmosphere.

Sgurr a'Mhadaidh Ruaidh towers pyramid-like above Loch Cuithir and the surrounding moorland, and from the loch is reached by first heading left of its cliffs to the ridge that forms the skyline. The ridge itself rises to unstable cliffs that must be avoided, but beyond a shallow corrie you find another ridge, broken, but more stable, and a way, albeit messy in places, up to the main ridge. Not surprisingly, the summit is a fine viewpoint, and well worth the effort.

Press on around the rim of Coir' an t-Seasgaich, a pleasant elevated walk, to reach Baca Ruadh.

The way back is a little sensational, and involves descending directly from the top of Baca Ruadh, down its steep eastern slope (grassy, and therefore slippery when wet) aiming to the right of Baca Ruadh's eastern buttress, and keeping to the grassy slopes throughout.

When you can do so, contour around the base of Baca Ruadh, cross the rough bounds of Coir' an t-Seasgaich, and the equally rugged base of Sgurr a'Mhadaidh Ruaidh, all the time heading back towards Loch Cuithir, and its ancient supply road.

WALK 6.12:
Inver Tote and the Lealt Waterfalls

Considering that it lies only 300m/yds from a busy road, the shore-line at Inver Tote can seem as remote as any place on Skye, and just as peaceful, with lazy waves lapping the stony beach and the occasional salmon finding its way into the mouth of the Lealt River.

As the river passes beneath the A855 so it drops over a rock lip to form an impressive waterfall, but this cannot be seen from the road. This brief walk takes you down to the shoreline, and is very steep with airy views both of the waterfall and its gorge.

Start/Finish: Roadside car park, A855, near turning to Lealt. GR.516605.
Distance: 1km (½ mile).
Ascent: 80m (260 feet).

Cross the fence beside the car park and follow a path around the edge of the gorge to reach a disused quarry that supplied material for adjoining road improvements. If you keep to the right of the quarry you can approach, with care, the upper rim of the gorge, for a good view of the waterfalls.

At the back of the quarry a path leads down to a broad, sloping grassy ledge (slippery when wet) from the edge of which you can look down into the gorge. Continue down the grassy slope and as the shore below comes into view, so does a path zigzagging down the slope that remains.

Eventually, you reach some old steps, rather overgrown, that lead you down to the old building, completely unsuspected from above, that used to dry diatomite from Loch Cuithir before shipment.

This small spot, rarely visited, with its seaward views decorated by wheeling gulls, fulmars and gannets, is a peaceful haven, well suited to wasting time.

WALK 6.13:
Bearreraig Bay

Quite unsuspected, rarely visited, Bearreraig Bay is the first place along the coast north of Portree where you can get down to the shoreline, but it is not a walk for the faint-hearted for it involves the descent (and subsequent re-ascent) of 640 concrete steps. The justification for such effort is a fine waterfall, a tranquil refuge (often a sun trap), a fine view of Holm Island, once thought to be the Celtic Paradise, and a wealth of small fossils.

Start/Finish: The Storr car park. GR.509529.
Distance: 4km (2½ miles).
Ascent: 170m (555 feet).

Although it means a little road-walking, parking at the Storr car park is the most convenient starting point. Go down the road to the southern edge of the forest, and turn left along the access road to the Storr Lochs dam. Follow the access road, and cross the dam to a cottage. From the cottage a pulley-operated railway descends to an electricity generating station sensibly concealed out of sight on the bay. Accompanying the railway is a never-ending flight of steps; go down them and pass round the power station to reach the stony beach, set in a fine sweep below towering basalt cliffs.

If you go to the right as you reach the beach you will have a view of humped Holm Island, standing off-shore in splendid isolation, while to the left you see the waterfall flowing from the dam. The beach itself is a good place to look for ammonites, small circular fossils in the rocks.

Holm Island was once believed to be Tir-nan-h'Oig, the Land of Perpetual Youth, the Celtic Paradise. Opposite Holm Island

Berreraig Bay, north of Portree – "a tranquil refuge"

workmen constructing the Trotternish road found a large underground passage built of stone and stone-roofed in which the bones of prehistoric animals were found along with flint weapons.

Among the bizarre events alleged to have happened on Skye was the Rite of Taghairm, which involved the roasting of live cats to raise the Devil. The rite is thought to have last been performed at Bearreraig, in an attempt to divine the future.

When you have explored sufficiently, you have those steps to deal with before the mercy of the access road.

Treasure Trove

One of the most noticeable instances of the discovery of treasure trove occurred in Bearreraig Bay in 1891, when a hoard of 28 objects of silver was discovered, including neck rings, brooches, bracelets and ingots. Ninety-two Anglo-Saxon pennies dating from the tenth century were also found, along with 18 silver coins (Kufic dirhems) of the Samanid Caliphs, struck at Samarkand. The most likely explanation was that the hoard had been concealed by a Norse seafarer.

WALK 6.14:
Sithean Bhealaich Chumhaing

With a commanding view of the island of Raasay, Ben Tianavaig to the south and the distant pinnacles of The Storr to the north, the cliffs north of Portree Bay rise dramatically, but for the most part unseen, to the grassy height of Sithean Bhealaich Chumhaing. The walk not only takes in this modest height, but uses the occasion to visit an ancient dun and isolated Ben Chracaig, which shares with Vriskaig Point the task of harbouring the waters of Portree.

The walk goes through an unprotected area invariably grazed by sheep and cattle, and for that reason dogs should not be taken. **The walk is not advised in poor visibility.**

Start/Finish: Portree Bay, north shore, near Coolin Hills Hotel. GR.487438. Take the minor road, off the Trotternish road, signposted to Budhmor.
Distance: 10km (6¼ miles).
Ascent: 400m (1315 feet).

Set off along the shore path, continuing round the headland at Sgeir Mhor where the steep profile of Sithean Bhealaich Chumhaing comes into view. Round the headland the path passes beneath Ben Chracaig which will later conclude the walk.

Gradually the path ascends through boulders, away from the shore to a wall and gate giving access to the Bile, a grassy ledge that is geologically a raised beach. Through the gate go through the ensuing pasture to another gate, and go through this also. Now a rough path beside a fence leads to a stile at the top of the field, where you also meet the track to Torvaig. Keep ahead across a sloping field, and over a dilapidated wall to a small burn and a fence.

Keep the fence on your right, and follow it to a hill gate and stile. Cross the stile and use on-going sheep tracks through steep heather-clad slopes to move out to the cliff top. The stretch northwards to distant Sithean Bhealaich Chumhaing is not as long as it seems, and enriched by pleasant airy walking and stupendous views, but do take care near the cliff edge. The top of Sithean Bhealaich Chumhaing is marked by a trig station, and on a fine day is an excellent place to take a prolonged break.

The return journey, which begins by retracing your route to the hill gate and stile, faces directly towards the dark Cuillin skyline, the Red Hills and the Cuillin Outliers, all dominated by the towering cliff profile of Ben Tianavaig and the glistening waters of the Sound of Raasay.

From the hill gate/stile, instead of retracing your steps, follow the line of a fence on your right until you meet the track to Torvaig. Follow this through a gate and up to the houses at Torvaig, following the road round and go through sheep pens and sheds. When clear of these you can either keep ahead, descending easily on a path to the Coolin Hills Hotel, or turn left and climb the trackless hillside to Dun Torvaig. The dun was once a prominent fortification and look-out post but now, as most on the Island, little more than a roughly-shaped pile of stones.

Cross Dun Torvaig and go towards the cliff top and Ben Chracaig, there following the cliff top around the headland, finally descending steeply to the boathouse on Portree Bay.

WALK 6.15:
Glen Varrigill Forest Walk

The brief woodland walk begins at the splendid Skye Heritage Centre, which not only provides excellent refreshments, books and souvenirs, but has a fine audio-visual exhibition. In addition to the walk described here, from the car park you can follow the splendid Gaelic Alphabet Trail, along which trees represent letters from the Gaelic alphabet.

Start/Finish: Skye Heritage Centre. GR.477425.
Distance: 3km (2 miles).
Ascent: Nominal.

The walk follows a well-maintained path throughout, and begins from the car park. Go through a gate in a corner and climb the narrow path beyond. Many parts of the forest are densely shaded, but vistas open up from time to time of the Cuillin, Portree Bay and Ben Tianavaig.

The forest is a wonderful habitat for birds, flowers (but only those that can cope with the dense shade or find light where the canopy opens) and fungi.

The way is waymarked in white throughout, and brings you back to the heritage centre in about one hour.

WALK 6.16:
Ben Tianavaig

In spite of being a finely sculpted hill, both inspiring and beautiful, and visible from many parts of the Island, Ben Tianavaig tends to maintain a lonely vigil above the Sound of Raasay, seldom visited by walkers. The eastern side of the hill collapses in the landslip manner characteristic of the Trotternish Ridge summits, while the western aspect is one of bleak peat moorland.

This walk makes a fine ascent along the cliff edge to the top of Tianavaig, and offers an alternative return by descending to the shore and following the coastline back to Tianavaig Bay. Although there are no paths, the going is quite easy underfoot and makes use of many sheep tracks, and the whole outing is considerably more pleasant than might be imagined.

Start/Finish: Camastianavaig. Park opposite Tianavaig Bay. GR.508389. Leave the main Portree road near the Abhainn Varrigill and take the Braes road (B883). Turn down to Tianavaig Bay.
Distance: 8km (5 miles).
Ascent: 410m (1345 feet).

From the bay walk north a short distance to the second bend and leave the road at the post box through a fenced break between bungalows (signposted: Creagan) and a stand of trees. Keep on through the break to a boundary fence partially concealed by bracken (Beware barbed wire) beyond which lies the open moor. Go left for a short distance above the fence and then start to cross the moor, trending left up a steep heathery brae, and through a low band of rocks. Cross another outburst of rocks and then head for a pronounced lump ahead, which proves to be on the cliff edge.

As you reach the lump the scenery is breathtaking, as good as any on Skye.

Along the cliff edge the tussling tussocks of the moor give way to close-cropped turf that eases the steady climb to the trig on the summit. If time is of the essence, you will retrace your steps.

Otherwise, gaze down into a sloping basin below the summit, for this is the way you are going, though not directly. Go north from the summit, round and down to a grassy bealach on the upper edge of the hollow. Continue round the hollow, keeping to the outer edges to avoid rough and bouldery going in the middle, and pass a pinnacle of rock of the same origin as those found around The Storr and the Quiraing. Here keep on across the hollow. As you reach the other side follow more sheep tracks out of this little amphitheatre and down steep grassy slopes to the shore.

A good path now leads you along the shore to Tianavaig Bay. As you pass below Creagan na Sgalain the path scampers beneath a small rock outcrop, after which you can descend to the shoreline and follow it round to your starting point. If the tide plays havoc with this plan, go behind the nearby houses to rejoin your outward path.

WALK 6.17:
The Braes

The isolated community of The Braes can most easily be reached by car, by a long minor road that leaves the main Portree road near the Abhainn Varrigill. For a more extended walk you can follow the north shore of Loch Sligachan to the road end at Peinchorran, and continue from there to the tip of An Aird at Dunan an Aislidh.

Start/Finish: Sligachan campsite. GR.485303.
Distance: 16km (10 miles), if you walk to the dun and back.
Ascent: Nominal.

Follow the good path that leaves a corner of the campsite and heads along the northern shore of Loch Sligachan. When you reach the end of the path, take to the road and soon branch right on a second road, leaving this to cross rough ground to the promontory.

Virtually all of the coastline around Balmeanach Bay is worth exploring before retracing your steps.

The Battle of the Braes

On the morning of 17 April 1882, a force of Glasgow constables and others marched on The Braes intent on arresting agitating crofters who had reached boiling point when summonsed for grazing on land that had been theirs for generations. Many of the menfolk were away fishing, but those that remained were joined by the women who "fought like Amazons and several of them...severely mauled". In the running battle, waged with truncheons, sticks and stones, many a body was badly bruised before the police succeeded in taking their prisoners away to Portree.

As a result of this turmoil, a Royal Commission was set up by the Gladstone government in 1883 under the Chairmanship of Lord Napier, to inquire into the condition of the crofters. Working diligently and unstintingly, the Commission accumulated a mass of evidence and exposed "a state of misery, of wrong doing, and of patient long-suffering without parallel in the history of [the] country". The immediate consequence of the inquiry was the passing of the Crofters' Holdings Act in 1886, under the provisions of which fair rent and security of tenure were vouchsafed the smallholder.

Essential and Supplementary Reading

Bell's Scottish Climbs, J H B Bell (Gollancz, 1988)
50 Best Routes on Skye and Raasay, Ralph Storer (David and Charles, 1996)
The Charm of Skye, Seton Gordon (Cassell & Co. Ltd., 1st edition, 1929)
The Cuillin of Skye, B H Humble (The Ernest Press, 1952, Facsimile edition, 1986)
The Drove Roads of Scotland, A R B Haldane (House of Lochar, 1995)
The Famous Highland Drove Walk, Irvine Butterfield (Grey Stone Books, 1996)
From Wood to Ridge, Collected poems in Gaelic and English, Sorley MacLean (Vintage, 1991)
An Excursion Guide to the Geology of Skye, B R Bell and J W Harris (Geological Society of Glasgow, 1986)
The Geology of Skye, Paul Yoxon and Grace M Yoxon (Skye Environmental Centre, 1987)
The Heart of Skye, Jim Crumley (Colin Baxter Photography, 1994)
The Highland Clearances, John Prebble (Secker and Warburg, 1963, Penguin Books, 1969-1977)
History of Skye, Alexander Nicolson (Maclean Press, Portree, 2nd edition, 1994)
In Search of Scotland, H V Morton (Methuen & Co., 1929)
The Journal of a Tour to the Hebrides with Samuel Johnson LLD, James Boswell (J.M. Dent, London: Everyman, Ernest Rhys, ed., 1909)
The Lyon in Mourning, Rev Robert Forbes (Henry Paton, ed., Scottish Academic Press, Edinburgh, 1975, in Three Volumes)
Northern Lights: A Voyage in the Lighthouse Yacht to Nova Zembla and the Lord knows where in the summer of 1814, Sir Walter Scott (Ed. William F Laughlan, Byways Books, 1982)
On the Crofters' Trail, David Craig (Jonathan Cape, 1990)
Over the Sea to Skye: Ramblings in an Elfin Isle, Alasdair Alpin MacGregor (W & R Chambers Ltd., London and Edinburgh, 1930)
Portrait of Skye and the Outer Hebrides, W Douglas Simpson (Robert Hale, 1967-1973)
Prehistoric Skye, Paul Yoxon and Grace M Yoxon (Skye Environmental Centre, 1987)
Skye, Derek Cooper (Birlinn Ltd, Edinburgh, 1995)
Skye: The Island and its Legends, Otta F Swire (Blackie and Son Ltd., 2nd edition, 1973)
Skye: Walking, Scramblling and Exploring, Ralph Storer (David and Charles, 1989)
The Story of Scotland, Nigel Tranter (Lochar Publishing, Moffat, 1991)
Walks on the Isle of Skye, Mary Welsh (Westmorland Gazette, Kendal, 1990)

Glossary of Gaelic Words

aber mouth or confluence of a river
abhainn river
acarseid anchorage
achadh field or park
ailean green field
a(i)rd high promontory
airidh shieling
allt burn
aros house
ath ford

bac bank
b(h)a(i)gh bay
b(h)aile town
b(h)an white
barr top or summit
b(h)e(a)g little
bealach pass or col
bearn gap
beinne ben or hill
beithe birch tree
bo cow (plural ba)
bodach old man
bog soft damp
brae top summit
b(h)reac speckled
brua(i)ch steep hillside
b(h)uidhe yellow
burn stream

cailleach old woman
caisteal castle
cala(dh) harbour

camas channel or creek
caol kyle, strait narrow
carn, cairn pile of stones
cioch woman's breast
clach stone
clachan village
cladagh shore or beach
cladh churchyard
clais hollow
cleit ridge
cnap hillock
cnoc, cnok, knock small hill
coille wood forest
coire corrie
creag crag or cliff
cro sheep open
cruach stack heap

darach oak wood
dearg red
druim ridge
dubh black or dark
dun mound or fort

each horse
ear east
eas waterfall
eilach watercourse
eilean island

fada long
faich meadow
fank sheep pen
faoghail ford, sea channel
fasgadh shelter
fraoch heather
fuar cold
fuaran spring or well

garbh rough or harsh
geal bright
geo, geodha narrow cove
gil narrow glen
glais stream
glas grey or green
gleann glen or valley
gob point beak
gobhar goat

inbhir rivermouth, bay
iolaire eagle

lagan hollow
lairig pass or sloping face of a hill
leac flat stone
learg hillside
leathad slope or declevity
leathan broad
leitir slope
liath grey
linne sound or channel
loch lake
lon stream marsh

machair low grassy land
mam gently rising hill
maol headland
meadhon middle
meall rounded hill
mointeach moorland
mol shingly beach
monadh moor, hill
moine mossy
m(h)or large tall
mullach summit

ob bay, creek
odhar dappled
or gold
ord conical hill
os outlet of lake or river

poll, puill pond

ruadh red, reddish
rubha, rudha headland

sean old
sgarbh cormorant
sga(i)t skate
sgeir skerry
sgurr, sgorr peak
sith fairy
sithean fairy hill
slochd deep hollow
srath valley
sron promontory
stac stack
stob point
strath river valley
stuc pinnacle, peak
suidhe resting place

traigh beach
t(a)igh house
tulach hillock

uaimh cave
uig bay
uisge water, rain